SELF STUDY BIBLE COUR

Basic Edition

CW00663831

14 STUDIES THAT EXPLORE GOD'S WORD

SELF-STUDY
BIBLE
COURSE

DEREK PRINCE

Self Study Bible Course:
Basic Edition

© 1969, 2017 by Derek Prince Ministries, International

This edition published by Derek Prince Ministries-UK 2018

B91N SSBC
ISBN 978-1-78263-606-9

All Scripture quotations are taken from the King James Version of the Holy Bible.

The book *Foundational Truths for Christian Living,* © 1993, 2006 by Derek Prince
Ministries, International, which Derek Prince refers to in the *Self Study Bible Course,* is
published by Charisma House. Please refer to this book for further information and
study on the respective items.

Boldface type in Scripture quotations indicates the author's emphasis.

Derek Prince Ministries · www.derekprince.com

Set in Arno by Raphael Freeman, Renana Typesetting

CONTENTS

INTRODUCTION: INSTRUCTIONS TO THE STUDENT

Read these instructions before answering any questions

Almost anywhere in the world today where Christianity has come, we find some people who would like to be Christians – but they are weak, fearful, discouraged, defeated. In almost every case the reason is the same: such people have never learned to study the Bible for themselves and to apply its teaching in a practical way to their lives. That is why God says, in Hosea 4:6, *"My people are destroyed for lack of knowledge."* Once a person comes to know the truths of the Bible, and how to apply those truths in a practical way to his own life, the result is always the same: peace, victory, success, fruitfulness.

1. Purpose of this Bible Course

This Self Study Course has four main aims:

1. To provide you with a foundation of Bible knowledge on which you will be able to build a strong and successful Christian life;
2. To give you practice in searching the Scriptures, and in finding and claiming God's wonderful promises for yourself;

3. To train you in analyzing a passage of Scripture so as to find out for yourself its correct meaning;

4. To form in you the habit of accepting only those teachings about spiritual things which can be proved by direct reference to the Bible.

2. System of Bible References

The translation of the Bible used throughout this course is the King James ("Authorized") Version. This is the version most familiar and most easily available to English-speaking people all over the world. However, the great truths of Scripture taught in this course do not depend upon any one particular version, but would be equally clear in any other reliable version.

You must learn where to find each book in the Bible, and to understand the system of abbreviating the names of the books which is used throughout the course (for a detailed key to this system, see the "KEY TO ABBREVIATED NAMES OF BIBLE BOOKS" on page xv) References to passages of scripture are given as follows: first, the book; second, the chapter; third, the verse. For example, Rom. 3:23 indicates the Epistle to the Romans, chapter 3, verse 23. Again, 1 John 2:14 indicates the First Epistle of John, chapter 2, verse 14. In books that have no chapters, the verse number immediately follows the book. For example, 3 John 2 indicates the Third Epistle of John, verse 2.

3. How to Do the Studies

At the top of each question paper there is a short paragraph, headed "INTRODUCTION." This gives a brief summary of the main teaching contained in the questions that follow. Always read through the "INTRODUCTION" carefully before attempting to answer the questions.

In the first question paper, "STUDY NO. 1: GOD'S PLAN OF SALVATION," there are 22 questions. In parentheses, after each question, there are references to one or more passages of Scripture. The answer to each question is always to be found in the passages referred to in the parentheses after that question. Following after each question, there is a space, indicated by one or more lines, in which you must write your answer to the question. The correct procedure for answering the questions is as follows:

1. Read the question carefully.
2. Find the Scripture passages referred to in parentheses and read through these passages carefully, until you find the answer to that question.
3. In the space indicated by the lines, write down in brief simple language the answer which you have found.

Sometimes the answer to one question must be divided up into two or more parts. In such cases, the spaces for each part of the answer are numbered

(1) _____ (2) _____ (3) _____

etc., and each part of the answer must be written in the correct numbered space.

To make all this quite plain, we give you here the first two questions of Study No. 1, with the correct answers written in, to show you how and where to write your answers:

1. For what purpose were all things created? (Rev. 4:11)

For God's pleasure _____

2. Write down three things which God is worthy to receive. (Rev. 4:11)

(1) Glory _____ (2) Honor _____ (3) Power _____

When doing these questions for yourself, do not merely write down the answers given above. First, look up the Scripture passages for yourself, and work out your own answers. Then check your answers with the ones given above, to see if they are correct. Then carry on answering the rest of the questions in the same way, until you have completed the whole Study.

4. Memory Work

At the beginning of each question paper, there is a passage given for memory work. You must learn this passage by heart. This is how to proceed:

Take a blank card and on one side neatly print the study number in the top left-hand corner, and then the Scripture reference in the middle, followed by the study title. Here is how your first card should look, for example:

> Study No. 1
> Rom. 6:23
> God's Plan of Salvation (1)

Then, on the other side of the card, neatly write the Scripture passage itself, as follows:

> *"For the wages of sin is death; but the gift of God is eternal life through Jesus Christ our Lord."*

Carry your memory cards with you. Whenever you have a spare moment during the day, take the opportunity to review your memory verses. Regular review is the secret of successful memory work. In this way, you will not only learn the Word by heart, but the Word will be in your heart, giving you guidance, strength, spiritual food, victory over the devil, and seed to sow in the hearts of others.

When repeating the passage to be memorized, always begin and end by saying the reference to the book, chapter, and verse. For instance, the first memory passage should be repeated as follows: "Romans six, twenty-three. For the wages of sin is death; but the gift of God is eternal life through Jesus Christ our Lord. Romans six, twenty-three." In this way, you will not only memorize the passage but also its reference in the Bible. Thus, you will be able to find it easily at any time, whether for yourself or others.

5. Procedure for Working Through the Course

Write in your answer to every question in Study No. 1, and then – with your Bible closed – write out the memory work in the space provided at the end. Then turn over the page to the Correct Answers to this Study. Check your own answers by reference to these Correct Answers. If in any case your answer does not agree with the corresponding Correct Answer, read through both the question and the relevant Scripture passage again until you understand clearly the reason for the Correct Answer.

On the page opposite the Correct Answers, you will find Notes on these answers, which explain them more fully. Take time to read through these Notes, and to look up any further passages of Scripture referred to in them.

Finally, evaluate your own work by writing against each answer that you have given the mark you feel you deserve for that answer. A simple standard of marking is given together with the Correct Answers. If an answer is valued at more than one mark, do not allow yourself the full mark unless your answer is as complete as the Correct Answer. Remember that the marks for the Memory Work are important!

Add up your marks for Study No. 1 and check this total by reference to the three standards given at the bottom of the Correct Answers: 50 percent or more rates as a "Pass"; 70 percent or more as a "Credit"; 80 percent or more as a "Distinction."

When you have completed all that there is to do in connection with Study No. 1, turn over to Study No. 2, and work through this in the same way. Continue like this until you have completed the whole course. The methods for doing the last two studies – Nos. 13 and 14 – are slightly different, but they are clearly explained at the head of each Study.

Remember! You must *never* turn over to the Correct Answers for any study until you have first written in your own answer to every question in that Study – including the Memory Work!

When you have completed the last Study, turn over to the page headed "Marks for the Course." Write in your marks for each study in the space provided, add them up, and evaluate your standard of achievement for the course as a whole. However, you will find that the final evaluation cannot be expressed merely in terms of "marks," but only in terms of enduring spiritual blessings and achievements which will have come to you through faithfully working through the complete course.

6. Final Personal Advice

1. Begin each study with prayer, asking God to guide you and give you understanding.
2. Do not work too quickly. Do not try to accomplish the whole study at one sitting. Read through each passage of Scripture several times, until you are sure of its meaning. It will often be helpful to read several verses before or after the actual passage, in order to grasp its full meaning.
3. Write neatly and clearly. Do not make your answers longer than necessary. Use a well sharpened pencil or a ballpoint pen.
4. Pay special attention to the Memory Work.
5. Pray daily that God may help you to apply in your own life the truths that you are learning.

KEY TO ABBREVIATED NAMES OF BIBLE BOOKS

Books of the Old Testament

I. THE LAW

Genesis	– Gen.
Exodus	– Ex.
Leviticus	– Lev.
Numbers	– Num.
Deuteronomy	– Deut.

II. HISTORY

Joshua	– Josh.
Judges	– Jud.
Ruth	– Ruth
1 Samuel	– 1 Sam.
2 Samuel	– 2 Sam.
1 Kings	– 1 Kin.
2 Kings	– 2 Kin.
1 Chronicles	– 1 Chron.
2 Chronicles	– 2 Chron.
Ezra	– Ezra
Nehemiah	– Neh.
Esther	– Est.

III. POETICAL BOOKS

Job	– Job
Psalms	– Ps.
Proverbs	– Prov.
Ecclesiastes	– Ecc.
Song of Solomon	– Song

IV. MAJOR PROPHETS

Isaiah	– Is.
Jeremiah	– Jer.
Lamentations	– Lam.
Ezekiel	– Ezek.
Daniel	– Dan.

V. MINOR PROPHETS

Hosea	– Hos.
Joel	– Joel
Amos	– Am.
Obadiah	– Ob.
Jonah	– Jon.
Micah	– Mic.
Nahum	– Nah.
Habbakuk	– Hab.
Zephaniah	– Zeph.
Haggai	– Hag.
Zechariah	– Zec.
Malachi	– Mal.

Books of the New Testament

I. GOSPELS

Matthew	– Matt.
Mark	– Mark
Luke	– Luke
John	– John

II. HISTORY

Acts	– Acts

III. PAULINE EPISTLES

Romans	– Rom.
1 Corinthians	– 1 Cor.
2 Corinthians	– 2 Cor.
Galatians	– Gal.
Ephesians	– Eph.
Philippians	– Phil.
Colossians	– Col.
1 Thessalonians	– 1 Thess.
2 Thessalonians	– 2 Thess.
1 Timothy	– 1 Tim.
2 Timothy	– 2 Tim.
Titus	– Tit.
Philemon	– Philem.
Hebrews	– Heb.

IV. GENERAL EPISTLES

James	– Jam.
1 Peter	– 1 Pet.
2 Peter	– 2 Pet.
1 John	– 1 John
2 John	– 2 John
3 John	– 3 John
Jude	– Jude

V. PROPHECY

Revelation	– Rev.

(Note that "John" stands for the Gospel of John, but "1 John" for the First Epistle of John, and so on.)

GOD'S PLAN OF SALVATION

Introduction:

Sin is an inward spiritual attitude of rebellion towards God, which is expressed in outward acts of disobedience. We are all sinners in this way, and by our sinful lives we rob God of the glory due to Him. Sin is followed by three main consequences: first, inward spiritual death, or alienation from God; second, the physical death of the body; third, final and eternal banishment from the presence of God to a place of darkness and torment. Christ came to save us from our sins. Himself without sin, He took our sins upon Him, died in our place, and rose again from the dead, that we might be forgiven and receive eternal life.

Memory Work: Rom. 6:23

Please check when memory card prepared ☐

A. Sin and Its Consequences

1. For what purpose were all things created? (Rev. 4:11)

   _____ For God's Pleasure _____

2. Write down three things which God is worthy to receive. (Rev. 4:11)

   (1) _glory_   (2) _honour_   (3) _power_

3. In what way have all men sinned? (Rom. 3:23)

We have all come short of the glory of God

4. When men turned away from God, what were the first two
   sins that they committed? (Rom. 1:21)

(1) didn't recognize him as God

(2) were not grateful

5. What were the results of this? (Rom. 1:21)

(1) In man's mind? they became vain

(2) In man's heart? their heart was darkened

6. Write down two facts about the human heart. (Jer. 17:9)

(1) deceitful

(2) wicked

7. Who alone knows the truth about the human heart? (Jer.
   17:10)

I, the Lord

8. Write down thirteen evil things that come out of the human
   heart. (Mark 7:21–22)

(1) adultery   (2) blasphemy

(1) fornication   (2) pride

(3) murder   (4) foolishness

(5) theft   (6) an evil eye

(7) covetousness   (8) evil thoughts

(9) wickedness   (10)

(11) deceit   (12)

(13) lasciviousness

2

9. If we are able to do something good, and we do not do it, what does God call that? (James 4:17)

Sin

10. If we say that we have no sin, what are we doing to ourselves? (1 John 1:8)

We deceive ourselves and the truth is not in us

11. If we say that we have not sinned, what are we doing to God? (1 John 1:10)

We make him a liar and his word is not in us

12. What consequence has sin brought upon all men? (Rom. 5:12; 6:23; Jam. 1:15)

death

13. What is the final end of all unrepentant sinners? (Matt. 25:41; Rev. 20:12–15)

the everlasting fire, the lake of fire — HELL

14. Write down eight different kinds of people who will go to the lake of fire. (Rev. 21:8)

(1) _fearful_   (2) _unbelieving_

(3) _abominable_   (4) _murderers_

(5) _whoremongers_   (6) _sorcerers_

(7) _idolaters_   (8) _liars_

B. The Purpose of Christ's Death and Resurrection

15. For what purpose did Christ come into the world? (1 Tim. 1:15)

   To save sinners ✓

16. Whom did Christ call and whom did He receive? (Matt. 9:13; Luke 15:2)

   He received sinners
   He called sinners to repentance ✓

17. Did Christ Himself commit any sins? (Heb. 4:15; 1 Pet. 2:22)

   No, tempted but without sin ✓

18. What did Christ bear in for us on the cross? (1 Pet. 2:24)

   He bore our sins ✓

19. For what purpose did Christ die on the cross? (1 Pet. 3:18)

   Christ died that he might bring us to God ✓

20. What three facts about Christ did Paul teach as the gospel? (1 Cor. 15:3–4)

   (1) _Christ died for our sins according to the scriptures_ ✓
   (2) _that he was buried_ ✓
   (3) _that he rose again according to the scriptures_ ✓

21. Seeing that Christ is now alive forevermore, what is He able to do for those who come to Him? (Heb. 7:25)

   Christ is still able to save people forevermore ✓

4

22. Write down three things now offered to all men in the name of Jesus. (Luke 24:47; Acts 4:12)

(1) _repentance_

(2) _remission of sins / Salvation_

(3) _eternal life._

Memory Work: Romans 6:23

Write out this verse from memory.

For the wages of sin is death, but God's free gift is eternal life in union with Christ Jesus our Lord.

DO NOT TURN THIS PAGE UNTIL YOU HAVE COMPLETED ALL ANSWERS IN THIS STUDY

STUDY NO. 1: GOD'S PLAN OF SALVATION

Correct Answers and Marks

Question	Answers	Marks
1.	For God's pleasure	1
2.	(1) Glory (2) Honor (3) Power	3
3.	All have come short of the glory of God	1
4.	(1) They did not glorify God (2) They were not thankful	2
5.	(1) They became vain in their imaginations	1
	(2) Their foolish heart was darkened	1
6.	(1) It is deceitful above all things	1
	(2) It is desperately wicked	1
7.	The Lord (God)	1
8.	(1) Evil thoughts (2) Adulteries (3) Fornications	3
	(4) Murders (5) Thefts (6) Covetousness (7) Wickedness	4
	(8) Deceit (9) Lasciviousness (10) An evil eye	3
	(11) Blasphemy (12) Pride (13) Foolishness	3
9.	God calls that Sin	1
10.	We are deceiving ourselves	1
11.	We are making God a liar	1
12.	Death	1
13.	Everlasting fire – the lake of fire – the second death	1
14.	(1) The fearful (2) The unbelieving (3) The abominable	3
	(4) Murderers (5) Whoremongers (6) Sorcerers	3
	(7) Idolaters (8) All liars	2
15.	To save sinners	1
16.	Christ called and received sinners	1
17.	None	1
18.	Our sins	1
19.	To bring us to God	1
20.	(1) Christ died for our sins (2) He was buried	2
	(3) He rose again the third day	1
21.	To save them to the uttermost	1
22.	(1) Repentance (2) Remission of sins (3) Salvation	3

Consult Bible for written Memory Work
If word perfect, 4 marks   4
(1 mark off for each mistake. If more than 3 mistakes, no marks.) ____

TOTAL 54

50% – 27   70% – 38   80% – 43

Notes on Correct Answers

(The numbers in the left-hand margin correspond to
the numbers of the correct answers on the previous page.)

1–4. Basically, man's sin is his failure to fulfill his God-given func-
tion. Man was created to glorify God. "*He is the image and glory
of God*" (1 Cor. 11:7). Any behavior of man that fails to glorify
God is sinful.

3. "*Come short of the glory of God.*" The picture is taken from an
arrow shot at a mark, but falling short of it. The "mark" of man's
existence is "*the glory of God.*" But all have fallen short of this
mark. (Compare Phil. 3:14.)

6–8. All these Scriptures speak about "*the heart*" generally. They
describe the inward condition of all fallen humanity, without
any exceptions.

8. Not all these sins here mentioned are actually committed by
all men. But the "*seeds*" of all these sins are found in every
heart. Character and circumstances, combined, decide which
of these "*seeds*" will actually bring forth the corresponding
actions in any individual life.

9. Many people are guilty not so much for what they "commit"
as for what they "omit." In Matt. 25:3, 25, 45, the foolish virgins, the unfaithful steward, and the "goat" nations are all
condemned for what they did not do.

13. We must distinguish two different places: (1) "Hell" (Hebrew
sheol; Greek *hades*): a place of confinement for departed
souls, prior to resurrection and judgment (Luke 16:23).

(2) "Gehenna" or "the lake of fire": a place of final, unending punishment for the wicked, after resurrection and judgment. (See Rev. 20:12–15).

14. Note the first two classes of the condemned: the "fearful" and the "unbelieving." How many "religious" people are included?

18. *"Now once in the end of the world hath he* [Christ] *appeared to put away sin by the sacrifice of himself"* (Heb. 9:26). By the sacrifices of the law of Moses sin was temporarily "covered." (See Heb. 10:1–4.) By the death of Christ sin was finally "put away." (See Heb. 10:11–18.)

19. Unforgiven sin is the great barrier between God and man. (See Is. 59:2.) When sin was put away by Christ on the cross, the way was opened for man to come back to God. Any barriers that now remain are on man's side, not on God's.

20. "Faith" is built on "fact." The "gospel" is based on these three simple, historical facts.

21. "To the uttermost" includes every need of every sinner in time and eternity. Christ is sufficient for all.

GOD'S PLAN OF SALVATION
(CONTINUED)

Introduction:

God now offers salvation to us not through any religion or good works, but through our personal faith in Christ. In order to be saved, we must acknowledge our sins and repent (that is, turn from our sins); we must believe that Christ died for us, and rose again; we must receive the risen Christ by faith as our personal Savior, and we must publicly confess Him as our Lord. After we have received Christ in this way, He dwells continually in our hearts by faith, and He gives us eternal life and the power to lead a life of righteousness and victory over sin.

Memory Work: John 1:12–13
Please check when memory card prepared ☐
(Review daily Rom. 6:23)

C. How We May Receive Salvation

23. When should we seek salvation? (Prov. 27:1; 2 Cor. 6:2)

_____

24. Can we save ourselves by our own good works? (Eph. 2:8–9; Tit. 3:5)

_____

25. Can we be saved by keeping the law? (Rom. 3:20)

_____

26. If we desire God's mercy, what two things must we do? (Prov. 28:13)

(1) _____

(2) _____

27. If we confess our sins, what two things will God do for us? (1 John 1:9)

(1) _____

(2) _____

28. What is God's remedy to cleanse our hearts from all sin? (1 John 1:7)

_____

29. If we desire to be saved, what two things must we do? (Rom. 10:9–10)

(1) With our hearts? _____

_____

(2) With our mouths? _____

_____

30. If we come to Christ will He reject us? (John 6:37)

_____

31. If we open our hearts to receive Christ, what promise has He given us? (Rev. 3:20)

_____

32. If we receive Christ, what does He give us? (John 1:12)

_____

33. What experience do we have as a result? (John 1:13)

_____

34. When we receive Christ, what does God give us through Him? (Rom. 6:23)

_____

35. Is it possible for us to know that we have eternal life? (1 John 5:13)

_____

36. What record does God give us concerning Christ? (1 John 5:11)

_____

37. If we have received Jesus Christ, the Son of God, what do we have? (1 John 5:12)

_____

D. Salvation Gives Power to Overcome the World and the Devil

38. After we have received Christ, who lives in our hearts by faith? (Gal. 2:20; Eph. 3:17)

_____

39. What can we do through the strength which Christ gives us? (Phil. 4:13)

_____

40. If we confess Christ before men, what will He do for us? (Matt. 10:32)

_____

_____

41. If we deny Christ before men, what will He do for us? (Matt. 10:33)

_____

_____

42. What kind of person is able to overcome the world and its temptations?

(1) (1 John 5:4) _____

(2) (1 John 5:5) _____

43. Why are God's children able to overcome the world? (1 John 4:4)

_____

_____

44. By what two things do the people of God overcome Satan? (Rev. 12:11)

(1) _____

(2) _____

45. Whom has God promised to receive in heaven as His child? (Rev. 21:7)

_____

Memory Work: John 1:12–13
Write out these verses from memory.

_____

_____

_____

_____

_____

_____

DO NOT TURN THIS PAGE UNTIL YOU HAVE COMPLETED ALL ANSWERS IN THIS STUDY

STUDY NO. 2: GOD'S PLAN OF SALVATION (CONTINUED)

Correct Answers and Marks

Question	Answers	Marks
23.	Now, today	1
24.	No	1
25.	No	1
26.	(1) Confess our sins (2) Forsake our sins	2
27.	(1) Forgive our sins (2) Cleanse us from all unrighteousness	2
28.	The blood of Jesus Christ, God's Son	1
29.	(1) Believe that God has raised Jesus from the dead	2
	(2) Confess Jesus as Lord	1
30.	No	1
31.	"I will come in"	1
32.	Power to become the sons of God	1
33.	We are born of God (= born again)	1
34.	Eternal life	1
35.	Yes (John wrote for that purpose)	1
36.	God has given us eternal life in Christ	2
37.	Eternal life	1
38.	Christ lives in our hearts	1
39.	All things (that God wishes us to do)	1
40.	He will confess us before His heavenly Father	1
41.	He will deny us before His heavenly Father	1
42.	(1) The one who is born of God (through his faith)	1
	(2) The one who believes that Jesus is the Son of God	1
43.	Because the one in them (= God) is greater than the one in the world (= the devil)	2
44.	(1) By the blood of the Lamb (= Christ)	1
	(2) By the word of their testimony	1
45.	Him that overcometh	1

Consult Bible for written Memory Work
If word perfect, 4 marks for each verse   8
(1 mark off for each mistake. If more than 3 mistakes in either verse,
no marks for that verse.)
                                                                    ____
                                                          TOTAL 40

     50% – 20   70% – 28   80% – 32

Notes on Correct Answers

(The numbers in the left-hand margin correspond to
the numbers of the correct answers on the previous page.)

24–25. The Bible rules out every attempt of man to save himself, or to make himself righteous, apart from the grace of God received through faith in Christ.

25. The law was not given to make man righteous, but to show man that he is a sinner, and that he cannot save himself. (See Rom. 3:20; 7:7–13.)

26. Merely to "confess" sin, without "forsaking" it, does not procure for man the mercy of God. (Compare Is. 55:7.)

27. When God forgives sin, He also cleanses the sinner's heart. Thus cleansed, the sinner does not continue committing the sins which he has confessed.

28. Apart from the blood of Christ, man has no remedy for his own sinful heart.

29. (2) "Confess Jesus as Lord." This is more accurate than the King James translation. (Compare 1 Cor. 2:3; Phil. 2:11.)

31. Note that the words of Jesus in Rev. 3:20 are addressed to a professing Christian Church (at Laodicea). But in spite of their profession, Christ Himself was left outside, seeking to gain admission. To how many Christian churches does this apply today? Christ's promise to "come in" is made to the individual, not to the congregation as a whole. The decision to receive Christ is always an individual matter.

32. "Power" – more correctly, "authority."

33.   John 3:1–7 tells us that "we must be born again." John 1:12–13 tells us how we can be born again (of God.) It is by receiving Christ as our personal Savior and Lord.

34.   In Rom. 6:23, notice the contrast; (a) "wages" = the due reward for the sins we have committed; (b) "gift" = the free, undeserved gift of God's grace.

38.   The Christian life continues as it begins, "by faith." "*As ye have received Christ Jesus the Lord, so walk ye in him*" (Col. 2:6). We receive Christ by faith. We walk in Christ by faith. (See 2 Cor. 5:7.)

39.   More literally: "*I can do all things through Christ in me giving me the power*" (Phil. 4:13).

40–41. Christ is "*the high priest of our profession* [or confession]" (Heb. 3:1). His high-priestly ministry on our behalf is limited by the extent to which we "confess" Him. (Compare Heb. 4:14 and 10:21–23.) In the last resort, we have only two alternatives: to "confess," or to "deny."

44.   "*By the blood of the Lamb and by the word of our testimony*" means that we testify personally to what the Word of God says that the blood of Christ does for us. Here are some of the great benefits received through the blood of Christ: (1) redemption (Eph. 1:7); (2) cleansing (1 John 1:7); (3) justification (Rom. 5:9); (4) sanctification (Heb. 13:12).

45.   Compare Rom. 12:21. In the last resort, there are only two alternatives: either to overcome, or to be overcome.

GOD'S PLAN FOR HEALING OUR BODIES

Introduction:

By turning away from God in disobedience, man lost the blessing and protection of God, and came under a curse and the power of the devil. In this way, the devil was able to bring upon man's body many forms of pain and weakness and sickness. However, God in His mercy still desires to bless man, and to save him not only from sin, but also from sickness. For this reason Christ on the cross bore not only our sins, but also our sicknesses. Therefore, by faith in Christ we may now receive physical healing for our bodies, as well as forgiveness and peace for our souls.

Memory Work: 1 Peter 2:24

Please check when memory card prepared ☐

(Review daily John 1:12–13)

A. General: Who Brings Sickness and Who Brings Health?

1. Who first deceived man, and tempted him to disobey God? (Gen. 3:1–13; 1 John 3:8; Rev. 12:9)

_____

2. Why did pain, sickness and death first come to man? (Gen. 3:16–19)

_____

3. Who brought sickness upon Job? (Job 2:7)

_____

4. Who brought sickness on the woman here described, and how? (Luke 13:11, 16)

_____

5. Who oppresses people with sickness? (Acts 10:38)

_____

6. What does God promise to do for His people who obey Him? (Ex. 15:26)

_____

_____

7. What two things does God promise to do for His people who serve Him? (Ex. 23:25)

(1) _____

(2) _____

8. Do sicknesses belong to God's people or to their enemies? (Deut. 7:15)

_____

9. What two things did David say the Lord did for him? (Ps. 103:3)

(1) _____

(2) _____

18

10. What three things did the apostle John wish for his Christian friend? (3 John 2)

(1) _____

(2) _____

(3) _____

11. How many of God's promises may we claim through faith in Christ? (2 Cor. 1:19–20)

_____

12. For what purpose was Christ manifested to the world? (1 John 3:8)

_____

13. For what purpose did God anoint Christ with the Holy Ghost? (Acts 10:38)

_____

14. Whose will did Christ come to do? (John 5:30; 6:38)

_____

15. Who worked Christ's miracles in Him? (John 10:37–38; 14:10)

_____

16. How many did Christ heal of those who came to Him? (Matt. 8:16; 12:15; 14:35–36; Luke 4:40; 6:19)

_____

17. How many kinds of sickness did Christ heal? (Matt. 4:23–24; 9:35)

_____

18. When Christ did not heal many people, what was the reason? (Matt. 13:58; Mark 6:5–6)

_____

19. Does God ever change? (Mal. 3:6; James 1:17)

_____

20. Does Christ ever change? (Heb. 13:8)

_____

B. The Purpose of Christ's Death on the Cross

21. Mention three things which Christ bore in our place. (Matt. 8:17; 1 Pet. 2:24)

   (1) _____

   (2) _____

   (3) _____

22. As a result, what three consequences can we have in our lives? (1 Pet. 2:24)

   (1) _____

   (2) _____

   (3) _____

23. What was Christ made for us? (Gal. 3:13)

_____

24. From what has Christ redeemed us? (Gal. 3:13)

_____

25. How many kinds of sickness were included in the curse of the law? (Deut. 28:15, 21–22, 27–28, 35, 59–61)

_____

26. Which does God tell us to choose – blessing or curse? (Deut. 30:19)

_____

Memory Work: 1 Peter 2:24
(This verse refers to Christ)
Write out these verses from memory.

_____

_____

DO NOT TURN THIS PAGE UNTIL YOU HAVE COMPLETED ALL ANSWERS IN THIS STUDY

STUDY NO. 3: GOD'S PLAN FOR HEALING OUR BODIES

Correct Answers and Marks

Question	Answers	Marks
1.	The serpent – the devil – Satan	1
2.	Because man disobeyed God	1
3.	Satan – the devil	1
4.	Satan bound her with a spirit of infirmity	2
5.	The devil	1
6.	To put none of the diseases of Egypt upon them – to heal them	2
7.	(1) To bless their bread and water	1
	(2) To take sickness away from them	1
8.	To the enemies of God's people	1
9.	(1) The Lord forgave all his iniquities	1
	(2) The Lord healed all his diseases	1
10.	(1) That he might prosper (2) That he might be in health	2
	(3) That his soul might prosper	1
11.	All God's promises	1
12.	To destroy the works of the devil	1
13.	To do good and heal all who were oppressed by the devil	2
14.	The will of God the Father	1
15.	God the Father	1
16.	All – every one	1
17.	Every kind of sickness and disease	1
18.	The people's unbelief	1
19.	Never	1
20.	Never	1
21.	(1) Our infirmities (2) Our sicknesses (3) Our sins	3
22.	(1) We can be dead to sins	1
	(2) We can live unto righteousness	1
	(3) By His (Christ's) stripes we are healed	1
23.	A curse	1

Question	Answers	Marks
24.	The curse of the law	1
25.	Every kind of sickness	1
26.	Blessing	1

Consult Bible for written Memory Work
If word perfect, 4 marks 4
(1 mark off for each mistake. If more than 3 mistakes in either verse,
no marks for that verse.)

TOTAL 40

50% – 20 70% – 28 80% – 32

Notes on Correct Answers

(The numbers in the left-hand margin correspond to
the numbers of the correct answers on the previous page.)

1–2. Gen. 3 reveals the root cause of all human sufferings, and traces
it back to the devil. Jesus Himself said of the devil: "*He was a
murderer from the beginning*" (John 8:44).

3–5. If we trace all sickness back to its source, the devil is the sole
author of it. It is part of "the works of the devil."

6. An alternative translation: "I am Jehovah your Doctor." (See
Ex. 15:26.)

9. Note the repetition of "all" with both "iniquities" and "diseases."

10. Note that Gaius, to whom John wrote, was a model believer,
"walking in the truth" and "doing faithfully" his duty as a
believer. (See 3 John 3–5.)

11. Second Corinthians 1:20 rebuts dispensational theories which
would rob Christians of the benefits of physical healing in this
present dispensation. "*All*" God's promises are (*now*) for "*us*"
(= all Christians). Applied personally: "Every promise that
fits my situation and meets my need is for me now."

13. All three Persons of the Godhead are actively present in the

ministry of healing. The *Father* anointed the *Son* with the *Spirit*. The result: healing for all.

14–15. Christ is the perfect manifestation of God the Father's will. This applies to healing as to all else that Christ did.

16–18. There is no record in the gospels of any person who came to Christ for healing, who was not healed.

19–20. The unchanging truth of the gospel is based on the unchanging nature of God Himself.

21. Both Matthew and Peter are here quoting Is. 53:4–5. The correct literal translation of Is. 53:4 is: "Surely He has borne our sicknesses, and carried our pains." This refers to Christ. In 1 Peter 2:24, the word translated *"healed"* is the basic Greek word for physical healing, from which the Greek word for "doctor" is derived.

24. "The curse of the law" means the curse that results from the breaking of the law. This curse is fully described in Deut. 28:15–68. It includes every form of sickness.

26. God sets forth two opposite pairs: either (a) "life" and "blessing"; or (b) "death" and "cursing." It is left to man to choose.

GOD'S PLAN FOR HEALING OUR BODIES
(CONTINUED)

Introduction:

Healing for our bodies from God comes to us through hearing and believing God's Word, and through allowing God's Spirit to fill our bodies with the resurrection life of Christ. Not only may we receive healing for our own bodies in this way, but we may also offer healing and deliverance to others in the name of Jesus. Two main ways in which we may do this are by laying our hands on the sick and praying for them, or by getting believing church elders to anoint them with oil in the name of the Lord. If we act in faith in this way, God will work with us and confirm the truth of His Word by miracles of healing and deliverance.

Memory Work: Mark 16:17–18
Please check when memory card prepared ☐
(Review daily 1 Peter 2:24)

C. Three Means of Healing: (1) God's Word (2) God's Spirit (3) Our Faith

27. What does God send to heal and deliver us? (Ps. 107:20)

_____

28. Mention two things which God's words bring to His children. (Prov. 4:20–22)

(1) _____

(2) _____

29. If God's Spirit dwells in us, what will it do for our mortal bodies? (Rom. 8:11)

_____

30. What does God want to manifest in our mortal bodies? (2 Cor. 4:10–11)

_____

31. What did Jesus look for in those who came to Him for healing? (Matt. 9:28–29; Mark 2:5; 9:23; Luke 8:50)

_____

32. How did Peter explain the healing of a lame man? (Acts 3:16)

_____

_____

33. What did Paul perceive in the cripple at Lystra which enabled him to be healed? (Acts 14:8–10)

_____

34. How does faith come to us? (Rom. 10:17)

_____

D. The Authority Committed to Believers

35. Mention two kinds of power which Jesus the Messiah gave to His disciples. (Matt. 10:1)

    (1) _____

    (2) _____

36. Mention four things which Jesus commanded His disciples to do. (Matt. 10:8)

    (1) _____

    (2) _____

    (3) _____

    (4) _____

37. When the disciples failed to heal an epileptic, what two reasons did Jesus give? (Matt. 17:20–21; Mark 9:29)

    (1) _____

    (2) _____

38. What two things did Jesus say that a person who believed in Him would be able to do? (John 14:12)

    (1) _____

    (2) _____

39. What may believers do for sick people in the name of Jesus? (Mark 16:17–18)

    _____

    _____

40. What will happen to such sick people? (Mark 16:18)

    _____

41. What should a sick Christian do? (James 5:14)

_____

42. What two things should church elders do for a sick Christian?
(James 5:14)

(1) _____

(2) _____

43. What two things will the Lord do for such a Christian?
(James 5:15)

(1) _____

(2) _____

44. What kind of prayer will save the sick? (James 5:15)

_____

45. What two things did the disciples pray that God would do in
the name of Jesus? (Acts 4:30)

(1) _____

(2) _____

46. When the disciples went out and preached, what two things
did the Lord do for them? (Mark 16:20)

(1) _____

(2) _____

Memory Work: Mark 16:17–18

Write out these verses from memory.

_____

_____

_____

_____

_____

_____

DO NOT TURN THIS PAGE UNTIL YOU HAVE COMPLETED ALL ANSWERS IN THIS STUDY

STUDY NO. 4: GOD'S PLAN FOR HEALING OUR BODIES (CONTINUED)

Correct Answers and Marks

Question	Answers	Marks
27.	His (God's) word	1
28.	(1) Life (2) Health to all their flesh	2
29.	It will quicken (= give life to) our mortal bodies	1
30.	The life of Jesus	1
31.	Faith	1
32.	Faith in the name of Jesus had healed him	2
33.	The cripple had faith to be healed	1
34.	By hearing the word of God	2
35.	(1) Power over unclean spirits to cast them out	2
	(2) Power to heal all manner of sickness and disease	2
36.	(1) To heal the sick (2) To cleanse the lepers	2
	(3) To raise the dead (4) To cast out demons	2
37.	(1) Because of their unbelief	1
	(2) It could only come out through prayer and fasting	1
38.	(1) The works that He did (2) Greater works than these	2
39.	Believers may lay hands on the sick in the name of Jesus	1
40.	They will recover	1
41.	He should call for the elders of the church	1
42.	(1) Pray over him	1
	(2) Anoint him with oil in the name of the Lord (= Jesus)	1
43.	(1) Raise him up (2) Forgive him if he has committed sins	2
44.	The prayer of faith	1
45.	(1) Stretch forth His hand to heal	1
	(2) Grant signs and wonders to be done	1
46.	(1) The Lord worked with them	1
	(2) He confirmed the word with signs following	2

Consult Bible for written Memory Work

If word perfect, 4 marks for each verse   8

(1 mark off for each mistake. If more than 3 mistakes, no marks.)   ____

TOTAL 44

       50% – 22   70% – 31   80% – 35

Notes on Correct Answers

(The numbers in the left-hand margin correspond to
the numbers of the correct answers on the previous page.)

27–34. Psalm 33:6 describes the means used by God in creation: *"By the Word of the Lord . . . and by the breath* [= spirit] *of His mouth."* All creation is by the *Word* and the *Spirit* of God working together. The same is true of God's re-creative work of healing. This is done by His *Word* and His *Spirit* working together. The means by which we receive this work of healing is our *faith.*

28.   Proverbs 4:20–22. The alternative translation of "health" is "medicine." These verses are God's great "medicine bottle." However, this medicine must be taken according to the directions, which are fourfold: (1) *"Attend"*; (2) *"Incline thine ear"* (be humble and teachable); (3) *"Let them not depart from thine eyes"*; (4) *"Keep them in the midst of thine heart."* The four channels to receive God's Word as medicine are the mind, the ear, the eye and the heart.

30.   2 Corinthians 4:10–11. God's will is that the resurrection life of Christ should be "manifested" (= openly revealed) in our "mortal flesh." This is God's provision of healing, health and vitality for our bodies in this present life.

34.   Romans 10:17. First, God's Word produces "hearing." Then, out of "hearing" there develops "faith." The process of "hearing" is described in its four phases in Proverbs 4:20–21.

35–36. In the New Testament no one is ever sent out to preach without also being commissioned to heal and to deliver from evil spirits. With Matthew 10:8 compare Matthew 28:20: *"Teaching them to observe all things whatsoever I have commanded you: and, lo, I am with you always, even unto the end of the age* [this present age]." Christ made provision that exactly the same ministry which He instituted with the first twelve disciples should be continued unchanged by each succeeding generation of disciples until the end of the present age.

37. (2) Jesus Himself practiced fasting, and He expected His disciples to follow Him in this also. (See Matt. 6:16–18.) However, the disciples did not do this as long as Jesus ("the bridegroom") remained with them on earth. (See Mark 2:18–20.)

38. The ministry of Jesus is the pattern for all Christian ministry. The Holy Spirit, sent by Jesus after He had returned to the Father, performs these works, promised by Jesus, through His believing disciples.

39. The promises of Mark 16:17–18 apply generally to *"them that believe"* – to all believers.

39–44. For further teaching on this subject, see Derek Prince's *The Spirit-filled Believer's Handbook*, Part v, Laying On of Hands.

41. A sick Christian who does not call for the elders of the church is disobedient.

45. Acts 4:30 is still a pattern prayer for the Christian church.

THE BIBLE: THE WORD OF GOD

Introduction:

The Bible is God's own Word, His great gift to all men everywhere, to help them out of their sin and misery and darkness. The Bible is not an ordinary book, but the men who wrote it were inspired and moved by God's Holy Spirit to write exactly the truth as God gave it to them. Every word is true, filled with God's own power and authority. We should read our Bible as if it was God Himself speaking to us directly and personally. It will impart to us light, understanding, spiritual food and physical health. It will cleanse us, sanctify us, build us up, make us partakers of God's own nature. It will give us power and wisdom to overcome the devil.

Memory Work: 2 Tim. 3:16–17

Please check when memory card prepared ☐

(Review daily Mark 16:17–18)

1. What name did Jesus give to the Scripture? (John 10:35)

_____

2. What did Jesus say about the Scripture which shows its authority? (John 10:35)

_____

3. Write down two things which David tells us about God's Word.

(1) (Ps. 119:89) _____

(2) (Ps. 119:160) _____

4. How were the Scriptures originally given?

(1) (2 Tim. 3:16) _____

(2) (2 Pet. 1:20–21) _____

5. What kind of seed must a person receive into his heart in order to be born again and have eternal life? (1 Pet. 1:23)

_____

6. Write down four things for which the Scriptures are profitable to a Christian. (2 Tim. 3:16)

(1) _____ (2) _____

(3) _____ (4) _____

7. What is the final result in a Christian who studies and obeys God's Word? (2 Tim. 3:17)

_____

_____

8. What is the spiritual food which God has provided for His children? (1 Pet. 2:2; Matt. 4:4)

_____

9. How much did Job esteem God's words? (Job 23:12)

_____

10. When Jeremiah fed on God's Word, what did it become to him? (Jer. 15:16)

_____

11. How can a young Christian person lead a clean life? (Ps. 119:9)

   _____

12. Why should a Christian hide (store up) God's Word in his heart? (Ps. 119:11)

   _____

13. What two results does God's Word produce in young men when it abides in them? (1 John 2:14)

   (1) _____

   (2) _____

14. How did Jesus answer the devil each time He was tempted? (Matt. 4:4, 7, 10)

   _____

15. What is the sword which God has given to Christians as part of their spiritual armor? (Eph. 6:17)

   _____

16. In what two ways does God's Word show Christians how to walk in this world? (Ps. 119:105)

   (1) _____

   (2) _____

17. What two things does God's Word give to the mind of a Christian? (Ps. 119:130)

   (1) _____ (2) _____

18. What does God's Word provide for the body of a Christian who studies it carefully? (Prov. 4:20–22)

   _____

19. When God's people were sick and in need, what did God send to heal and deliver them? (Ps. 107:20)

_____

20. Write down four things, mentioned in the following verses, which God's Word does for His people.

    (1) (John 15:3; Eph. 5:26) _____

    (2) (John 17:17) _____

    (3) (Acts 20:32) _____

    (4) (Acts 20:32) _____

21. How does a Christian prove his love for Christ? (John 14:21)

_____

22. Whom did Jesus call His mother and His brethren? (Luke 8:21)

_____

23. How is God's love made perfect in a Christian? (1 John 2:5)

_____

24. Write down two results which follow in our lives when we claim the promises of God's Word. (2 Pet. 1:4)

    (1) _____

    (2) _____

Memory Work: 2 Timothy 3:16–17

Write out these verses from memory.

_____

_____

_____

_____

DO NOT TURN THIS PAGE UNTIL YOU HAVE COMPLETED ALL ANSWERS IN THIS STUDY

STUDY NO. 5: THE BIBLE: THE WORD OF GOD

Correct Answers and Marks

Question	Answers	Marks
1.	The Word of God	1
2.	It cannot be broken	1
3.	(1) It is settled forever in heaven	1
	(2) It is true from the beginning	1
4.	(1) By inspiration of God	1
	(2) Holy men of God spoke as they were moved by the Holy Ghost	2
5.	The incorruptible seed of God's Word	1
6.	(1) Doctrine (2) Reproof (3) Correction	3
	(4) Instruction in righteousness	1
7.	He is made perfect (= complete) – thoroughly furnished (= equipped) for all good works	2
8.	The Word of God	1
9.	More than his necessary food	1
10.	The joy and rejoicing of his heart	1
11.	By taking heed to it according to God's Word	1
12.	That he may not sin against God	1
13.	(1) It makes them strong	1
	(2) They overcome the wicked one (= the devil)	1
14.	He answered from the written Word of God	1
15.	The Word of God	1
16.	(1) It is a lamp to their feet (2) It is a light to their path	2
17.	(1) Light (2) Understanding	2
18.	Health to all his flesh	1
19.	His (God's) Word	1
20.	(1) It cleanses – washes, like clean water	1
	(2) It sanctifies (3) It edifies	2
	(4) It gives them their inheritance	1
21.	He has Christ's commandments and keeps them	1
22.	Those who hear the Word of God and do it	1

Question	Answers	Marks
23.	By keeping God's Word	
24.	(1) We are made partakers of the divine nature	1
	(2) We escape the corruption of this world	1

Consult Bible for written Memory Work

If word perfect, 4 marks for each verse   8

(1 mark off for each mistake. If more than 3 mistakes, no marks.)   ____

TOTAL 49

50% – 24   70% – 34   80% – 39

Notes on Correct Answers

(The numbers in the left-hand margin correspond to
the numbers of the correct answers on the previous page.)

1–2.   It is perfectly clear that Jesus accepted the Old Testament Scriptures, without question or reservation, as the inspired, authoritative Word of God. He based all His teachings on these Scriptures, and directed the whole course of His own life to obey and fulfill them.

3.   God's Word originates in heaven. Men were the channels through whom this Word was given, but God Himself is the source of it.

4.   (1) "By inspiration of God" = literally "God inbreathed." The words "breath" and "spirit" are the same, both in Hebrew and Greek. (For a full study of the inspiration and authority of the Bible see Derek Prince's book *The Spirit-filled Believer's Handbook*, Part I, Foundation for Faith.)

5.   The "incorruptible seed" of God's Word, received by faith in the heart and caused to germinate there by the Holy Spirit, brings forth divine, eternal, incorruptible life.

6–8.   Note: *"all scripture"* (2 Tim. 3:16), *"every word"* (Matt. 4:4). For full spiritual development, a Christian must study and apply the teachings of the whole Bible.

8–10. God's Word provides food suited to every stage of spiritual development: (1) *"milk"* for newborn babes (1 Pet. 2:2); (2) *"bread"* for those growing up (Matt. 4:4); (3) *"strong meat"* (full diet) for those who are *"of full age"* (spiritually mature) (Heb. 5:12–14).

11. *"By taking heed thereto,"* etc." i.e., by carefully applying the teaching of God's Word to every phase of his life.

12. Someone has said: "Either God's Word will keep you from sin, or sin will keep you from God's Word."

13–15. In Eph. 6:13–17, Paul lists six items of spiritual armor which provide the Christian with complete protection, but of them all there is only one weapon of attack, *"the sword of the Spirit."* It is the responsibility of each believer to "take" this sword.

16. Compare 1 John 1:7: *"If we walk in the light...."* The *"light"* by which we must walk is God's Word.

17–19. God's Word provides for the spirit, the mind and the body of the Christian.

20. (4) Only through God's Word do we come to know what is our rightful inheritance in Christ, and how to obtain that inheritance.

21–23. *"The keeping of God's Word is the supreme distinguishing feature which should mark you out from the world as a disciple of Christ."* "Your attitude toward God's Word is your attitude toward God Himself. You do not love God more than you love His Word. You do not obey God more than you obey His Word. You do not honor God more than you honor His Word. You do not have more room in your heart and life for God than you have for His Word." (*The Spirit-filled Believer's Handbook*, Part I, Foundation for Faith, p. 36.)

24. Through God's Word, believed and obeyed, God's own nature permeates the heart and life of the believer, replacing the old, corrupt, Adamic nature.

THE HOLY SPIRIT

Introduction:

In all His earthly ministry, Jesus was completely dependent upon the Holy Spirit. Before the Holy Spirit descended upon Him at the river Jordan, He never preached a sermon or performed a miracle. After that, all He did was by the power of the Holy Spirit. When He was about to leave His disciples, He promised that from heaven He would send the Holy Spirit to them in their turn, to be their Comforter and to supply all their spiritual needs. This promise was fulfilled on the day of Pentecost when they were all baptized in the Holy Spirit.

NOTE: The two English expressions "Holy Spirit" and "Holy Ghost" are two different ways of translating one and the same expression in the original Greek of the New Testament. There is therefore no difference in meaning between these two expressions.

Memory Work: Acts 2:38–39
Please check when memory card prepared ☐
(Review daily 2 Tim. 3:16–17)

1. With what did God the Father anoint Jesus for His earthly ministry? (Acts 10:38)

_____

2. What did John the Baptist see descend and abide upon Jesus? (John 1:32–33)

_____

3. What did Jesus say was upon Him, enabling Him to preach and to minister to those in need? (Luke 4:18)

_____

4. By what power did Jesus say He cast out devils? (Matt. 12:28)

_____

5. Whom did Jesus say He would send to His disciples from the Father after He Himself returned to heaven? (John 14:16, 26; 15:26)

_____

6. What two expressions does Jesus use to describe the Comforter?

(1) (John 14:17) _____

(2) (John 14:26) _____

7. Write down two things which Jesus says the Holy Spirit will do for the disciples. (John 14:26)

(1) _____

(2) _____

8. Write down another way in which Jesus says the Holy Spirit will help the disciples. (John 16:13)

_____

9. Write down two ways in which the Holy Spirit will reveal Jesus to His disciples.

(1) (John 15:26) _____

(2) (John 16:14) _____

10. After what did Jesus say that the disciples would receive power to become effective witnesses for Him? (Acts 1:8)

_____

11. What did John the Baptist tell the people that Jesus would do for them? (Mark 1:8)

_____

12. What promise did Jesus give to His disciples just before He ascended into heaven? (Acts 1:5)

_____

13. What did Jesus tell His disciples to do until this promise should be fulfilled? (Luke 24:49)

_____

_____

14. Upon what day was this promise to these disciples fulfilled? (Acts 2:1–4)

_____

15. Why could the Holy Spirit not be given to the disciples during the earthly ministry of Jesus? (John 7:39)

_____

16. After Jesus had returned to His position of glory at the right hand of God, what did He receive from the Father? (Acts 2:33)

_____

17. How could the unbelievers present know that Jesus had poured out the Holy Spirit upon His disciples? (Acts 2:33)

_____

18. What could these unbelievers hear the disciples doing through the power of the Holy Spirit? (Acts 2:7–8)

_____

19. Upon whom does God promise to pour out His Spirit at the close of this age? (Acts 2:17)

_____

20. To whom does Peter say that the promised gift of the Holy Spirit is made available? (Acts 2:39)

_____

_____

21. What good gift will God the Father give to all His children who ask Him for it? (Luke 11:13)

_____

Memory Work: Acts 2:38–39

Write out these verses from memory.

_____

_____

_____

_____

_____

_____

DO NOT TURN THIS PAGE UNTIL YOU HAVE COMPLETED ALL ANSWERS IN THIS STUDY

STUDY NO. 6: THE HOLY SPIRIT

Correct Answers and Marks

Question	Answers	Marks
1.	With the Holy Ghost and power	1
2.	The (Holy) Spirit	1
3.	The Spirit of the Lord	1
4.	By the Spirit of God	1
5.	The Comforter	1
6.	(1) The Spirit of truth (2) The Holy Ghost	2
7.	(1) He will teach you all things	1
	(2) He will bring all things to your remembrance whatsoever I have said unto you	2
8.	He will guide you into all truth	1
9.	(1) He shall testify of Me (Jesus) (2) He shall glorify Me (Jesus)	2
10.	After that the Holy Ghost is come upon you	1
11.	He shall baptize you with the Holy Ghost	1
12.	Ye shall be baptized with the Holy Ghost not many days hence	2
13.	Tarry ye in the city of Jerusalem, until ye be endued with power from on high	2
14.	The Day of Pentecost (*Shavuot*)	1
15.	Because Jesus was not yet glorified	1
16.	The promise of the Holy Spirit	1
17.	They could see and hear it	1
18.	Speaking in the tongues (languages) of the countries in which the unbelievers had been born	2
19.	Upon all flesh	1
20.	To you, and to your children, and to all that are afar off, even as many as the Lord our God shall call	3
21.	The Holy Spirit	1

Consult Bible for written Memory Work
If word perfect, 4 marks for each verse   8
(1 mark off for each mistake. If more than 3 mistakes, no marks.)   ____
TOTAL 38

50% – 19   70% – 27   80% – 30

Notes on Correct Answers

(The numbers in the left-hand margin correspond to
the numbers of the correct answers on the previous page.)

1–5.   The English word "Christ" is taken from a Greek word which
means "Anointed." It thus corresponds exactly to the Hebrew
title, "Messiah," which also means "Anointed." In historical
experience Jesus became the "Messiah," the "Anointed One,
when the Holy Spirit descended and abode upon Him, after
His baptism by John the Baptist. The title "Christ" or "Messiah"
indicates that the whole earthly ministry of Jesus was made
possible by the "anointing" of the Holy Spirit. It is God's purpose that the same "anointing" of the Holy Spirit should be the
abiding portion of all Christians. *"Now he which establisheth us
with you in Christ, and hath anointed us, is God"* (2 Cor. 1:21).
"But the anointing which ye have received of him abideth in you…"
(1 John 2:27). "Christians" are literally "anointed ones." For
effective Christian living, the disciple is as much dependent
upon the Holy Spirit as Jesus Himself was.

5–6.   "Comforter" = "Advocate" – "One called in alongside." The
same word is used of Jesus in 1 John 2:1. Christ pleads the
cause of the believer in heaven. The Holy Spirit, through the
believer, pleads the cause of the Christ on earth. (See Matt.
10:19–20.)

6–9.   In John 16:7 Jesus said, *"It is expedient for you that I go away:
for if I go not away, the Comforter will not come unto you; but
if I depart, I will send Him unto you."* When Jesus returned
to heaven and sent the Holy Spirit upon the disciples, they

immediately received a better knowledge and understanding of Jesus Himself than they had had all the time that He was actually present with them on earth. Thus the Holy Spirit fulfilled His ministry to reveal, interpret and glorify the person, the work and message of Christ.

11. John the Baptist's introduction of Jesus as the baptizer in the Holy Spirit is placed at the forefront of all four gospels. The New Testament places the greatest possible emphasis upon this aspect of Christ's ministry. The Christian Church should do the same.

12–13. The gospels close, as they open, with the promise of the baptism in the Holy Spirit.

15–16. By His death on the cross, Jesus purchased for every believer the gift of the Holy Spirit. (See Gal. 3:13–14.) After His resurrection and ascension, it was His unique privilege to receive this gift from the Father and to bestow it upon His disciples.

17–18. All through the New Testament the baptism in the Holy Spirit is attested by the supernatural evidence of speaking with other tongues.

18–21. At the close of this age God has promised a final, worldwide outpouring of the Holy Spirit. Every Christian has the scriptural right to ask for this gift.

RESULTS OF THE BAPTISM IN THE HOLY SPIRIT

Introduction:

The baptism in the Holy Spirit is a supernatural enduement with power from heaven to equip the believer for effective witness and service. It is attested by speaking in a language given by the Holy Spirit but unknown to the one speaking. It enables the Christian to build up his own spiritual life by direct and continual communion with God and is the gateway into a life in which both the gifts and the fruits of the Holy Spirit should be manifested. In the New Testament Church, this experience was considered normal for all believers.

Memory Work: Acts 2:17–18

Please check when memory card prepared ☐

(Review daily Acts 2:38–39)

1. What happened to the disciples on the Day of Pentecost (*Shavuot*) when they were all filled with the Holy Ghost? (Acts 2:4)

_____

_____

2. Through whose preaching did the people of Samaria come to believe in Jesus as Messiah? (Acts 8:12)

_____

3. When Peter and John came down to Samaria, how did they pray for the Christians there? (Acts 8:15)

_____

4. How did the Christians at Samaria receive the Holy Ghost? (Acts 8:17)

_____

5. How did Saul of Tarsus (Paul) receive the Holy Ghost? (Acts 9:17)

_____

6. As Peter was preaching to the people in the house of Cornelius, what happened to all who heard him? (Acts 10:44)

_____

7. How did Peter and his companions know that all these people in the house of Cornelius had received the Holy Ghost? (Acts 10:45–46)

_____

8. What question did Paul ask the disciples at Ephesus? (Acts 19:2)

_____

9. How did these disciples at Ephesus receive the Holy Ghost? (Acts 19:6)

_____

10. What happened after the Holy Ghost came on these disciples? (Acts 19:6)

_____

11. How much did Paul say that he himself spoke in tongues? (1 Cor. 14:18)

_____

12. Write down three things that a Christian does when he speaks in an unknown tongue. (1 Cor. 14:2, 4)

(1) _____

(2) _____

(3) _____

13. If a Christian prays in an unknown tongue, what part of him is then praying? (1 Cor. 14:14)

_____

14. How did Jesus say that true worshipers should worship God? (John 4:23–24)

_____

15. How does Jude exhort Christians to build themselves up in their faith? (Jude 20)

_____

16. When a Christian speaks in an unknown tongue, what may he pray for next? (1 Cor. 14:13)

_____

17. In a public meeting where there is no interpreter, how may a Christian speak in an unknown tongue? (1 Cor. 14:28)

_____

18. Did Paul say that he wished that all Christians spoke in tongues? (1 Cor. 14:5)

_____

19. How many Christians did Paul say may prophesy? (1 Cor. 14:31)

_____

20. Should Christians be ignorant about spiritual gifts? (1 Cor. 12:1)

_____

21. Make a list of the nine gifts of the Spirit. (1 Cor. 12:8–10)

(1) _____   (2) _____

(3) _____   (4) _____

(5) _____   (6) _____

(7) _____   (8) _____

(9) _____

22. Make a list of the ninefold fruit of the Spirit. (Gal. 5:22–23)

(1) _____ (2) _____ (3) _____

(4) _____ (5) _____ (6) _____

(7) _____ (8) _____ (9) _____

23. Should a Christian have spiritual gifts without spiritual fruit? (1 Cor. 13:1–2)

_____

24. Should a Christian have spiritual fruit without spiritual gifts? (1 Cor 12:31; 14:1)

_____

25. Write down three supernatural occurrences that will result from the outpouring of the Holy Spirit at the end of this age. (Acts 2:17)

(1) _____

(2) _____

(3) _____

26. Write down five different spiritual contributions that a believer may make at a meeting with fellow believers. (1 Cor. 14:26)

(1) _____ (2) _____ (3) _____

(4) _____ (5) _____

Memory Work: Acts 2:17–18

Write out these verses from memory.

_____

_____

_____

_____

_____

_____

DO NOT TURN THIS PAGE UNTIL YOU HAVE COMPLETED ALL ANSWERS IN THIS STUDY

STUDY NO. 7:
RESULTS OF THE BAPTISM IN THE HOLY SPIRIT

Correct Answers and Marks

Question	Answers	Marks
1.	They spoke with other tongues as the Spirit gave them utterance	2
2.	The preaching of Philip	1
3.	That they might receive the Holy Ghost	1
4.	They (i.e. Peter and John) laid their hands on them	1
5.	Ananias put his hands upon him	1
6.	The Holy Ghost fell on them all	1
7.	They heard them speak with tongues and magnify God	1
8.	"Have ye received the Holy Ghost since ye believed?"	1
9.	Paul laid his hands upon them	1
10.	They spoke with tongues and prophesied	1
11.	More than ye all (i.e. more than all the Christians at Corinth)	1
12.	(1) He speaks to God (not to men) (2) He speaks mysteries	2
	(3) He edifies himself	1
13.	His spirit	1
14.	In spirit and in truth	1
15.	By praying always in the Holy Ghost	1
16.	That he may interpret	1
17.	He may speak to himself and to God	1
18.	Yes	1
19.	All	1
20.	No	1
21.	(1) The word of wisdom (2) The word of knowledge	2
	(3) Faith (4) Gifts of healings	2
	(5) Working of miracles (6) Prophecy	2
	(7) Discerning of spirits (8) Divers kinds of tongues	2
	(9) Interpretation of tongues	1

Question	Answers		Marks
22.	(1) Love	(2) Joy	2
	(3) Peace	(4) Longsuffering	2
	(5) Gentleness	(6) Goodness	2
	(7) Faith	(8) Meekness	2
	(9) Temperance		1
23.	No		1
24.	No		1
25.	(1) Your sons and your daughters shall prophesy		1
	(2) Your young men shall see visions		1
	(3) Your old men shall dream dreams		1
26.	(1) A psalm	(2) A doctrine	2
	(3) A tongue	(4) A revelation	2
	(5) An interpretation		1

Consult Bible for written Memory Work
If word perfect, 4 marks for each verse 8
(1 mark off for each mistake. If more than 3 mistakes, no marks.) ____

TOTAL 59

50% – 29 70% – 41 80% – 47

Notes on Correct Answers

(The numbers in the left-hand margin correspond to
the numbers of the correct answers on the previous page.)

1. *"Out of the abundance of the heart the mouth speaketh"* (Matt.
12:34). The first outflow of the Holy Spirit is from the believer's
mouth.

2–4. Through the ministry of Philip, multitudes in Samaria had
been wonderfully saved and healed. But this was not sufficient
for the apostles. They expected all new converts to receive
the baptism in the Holy Spirit. This came to these converts in
Samaria through the ministry of Peter and John, as a separate
experience, subsequent to salvation.

5. Laying on of hands to impart the Holy Spirit was not confined to apostles. Ananias is merely called a *"disciple"* (Acts 9:10). Nor is laying on of hands always needed to impart the Holy Spirit. In Acts 2:2–4 and 10:44–46 the believers received without any laying on of hands.

8–10. At Ephesus, as at Samaria, these disciples received the baptism in the Holy Spirit as a separate experience, subsequent to salvation. As in Acts 2:4 and 10:46, their experience culminated in speaking with other tongues (and also, in this case, prophesying).

11–15. After receiving the baptism in the Holy Spirit, the primary use of speaking in another tongue is for personal worship and prayer. The believer does not understand with his mind what he is saying, but his spirit holds direct communion with God, and in this way he is able to edify (build up) himself.

16–17. Through the gift of interpretation Christians may come to know the meaning of an utterance previously given in an unknown tongue. In public meetings an utterance given out loud in an unknown tongue should normally be followed by the interpretation. If there is no one to interpret, the believer may speak in an unknown tongue "to himself and to God."

19. To "prophesy" is to speak by the supernatural inspiration of the Holy Spirit in a language understood by the speaker and by those spoken to.

21–24. There is an important logical distinction between "gifts" and "fruit." A gift is imparted and received by a momentary act. Fruit is cultivated by time and labor. (See 2 Tim. 2:6.) Consider the difference between a Christmas tree with its gifts, and an apple tree with its fruit. Spiritually, gifts are not a substitute for fruit, and fruit is not a substitute for gifts. God's provision is for all Christians to have both. (Note that "love" is never called a "gift.")

25–26. The full outpouring of the Holy Spirit always produces a variety of supernatural manifestations. Through these, Christians are able to minister to one another on a level higher than that of natural ability or education.

WORSHIP AND PRAYER

Introduction:

Prayer is the great means by which Christians come into the presence of God, to worship Him, and to receive from Him the guidance, the help, and the strength which they need at all times. Every Christian should set aside regular times each day to spend in personal prayer and Bible reading. The most powerful and influential person in the world is the Christian who knows how to pray and to get his prayers answered. To be able to pray in this way we must follow carefully the instructions of God's Word, which are set out in this study, and we must have the help of the Holy Spirit.

Memory work: John 15:7
Please check when memory card prepared ☐
(Review daily Acts 2:17–18)

1. What kind of people is God seeking? (John 4:23–24)

   _____

2. In whose prayer does the Lord delight? (Prov. 15:8)

   _____

3. What kind of prayer produces great results? (James 5:16)

   _____

4. If we wish God to hear our prayers, what 2 things must we do? (John 9:31)

(1) _____ (2) _____

5. By what may we enter boldly into the holy presence of God? (Heb. 10:19)

_____

6. With what 2 things should we enter God's presence? (Ps. 100:4)

(1) _____ (2) _____

7. What should a Christian do instead of worrying? (Phil 4:6)

_____

_____

8. In whose name should we pray, and with what motive? (John 14:13)

_____

9. Upon what 2 conditions may we ask for what we will from God? (John 15:7)

(1) _____

(2) _____

10. Write down 4 things, found in the following verses, which will hinder the answers to our prayers:

(1) (Ps. 66:18) _____

(2) (James 1:6–7) _____

(3) (James 4:3) _____

(4) (1 Pet. 3:7) _____

11. In order to overcome Satanic forces, what must we sometimes join with prayer? (Mark 9:29)

_____

12. In order to receive the things that we desire, what must we do when we pray? (Mark 11:24)

_____

13. If we have anything against other people when we pray, what must we do first? (Mark 11:25)

_____

14. If we forgive others when we pray, how will God deal with us? (Mark 11:26)

_____

15. If we do not forgive others, how will God deal with us? (Mark 11:25)

_____

16. If we pray according to the will of God, of what two things may we be confident? (1 John 5:14–15)

(1) _____

(2) _____

17. How did David say he would begin each day? (Ps. 5:3)

_____

18. At what three times did David decide to pray each day? (Ps. 55:17)

(1) _____ (2) _____ (3) _____

19. Apart from such regular times of prayer, how often should we pray? (Eph. 6:18; 1 Thess. 5:17)

_____

20. When we do not have strength or knowledge to pray aright, who helps us to pray according to God's will? (Rom. 8:26–27)

_____

21. If we are praying alone, what does Jesus tell us to do? (Matt. 6:6)

_____

22. How does Jesus say that this kind of prayer will be rewarded? (Matt. 6:6)

_____

23. If we meet with other Christians for prayer in the name of Jesus, what promise has Jesus given us? (Matt. 18:20)

_____

24. What should be our attitude toward other Christians with whom we pray? (Matt. 18:19)

_____

25. For whom should we pray especially? (1 Tim. 2:1–2)

_____

26. What position of the body does Paul here recommend for prayer? (1 Tim. 2:8)

_____

27. What two wrong mental attitudes must we guard against when praying? (1 Tim. 2:8)

(1) _____ (2) _____

28. What is the result of getting our prayers answered? (John 16:24)

_____

Memory Work: John 15:7
Write out this verse from memory.

_____

_____

_____

_____

DO NOT TURN THIS PAGE UNTIL YOU HAVE COMPLETED ALL ANSWERS IN THIS STUDY

STUDY NO. 8: WORSHIP AND PRAYER

Correct Answers and Marks

Question	Answers	Marks
1.	True worshipers, who will worship God in spirit and in truth	2
2.	The prayer of the upright	1
3.	The effectual fervent prayer of a righteous man	2
4.	(1) Worship God (2) Do God's Will	2
5.	By the blood of Jesus	1
6.	(1) Thanksgiving (2) Praise	2
7.	In everything by prayer and supplication with thanksgiving make known his requests to God	3
8.	In the name of Jesus, for God to be glorified	2
9.	(1) If we abide in Christ	1
	(2) If His words abide in us	1
10.	(1) If we "regard iniquity" (tolerate known sin) in our heart	1
	(2) If we waver and do not ask in faith	1
	(3) If we ask amiss, to gratify our own lusts	1
	(4) A wrong relationship between husband and wife	1
11.	Fasting	1
12.	Believe that we receive them (at the time of praying)	1
13.	We must forgive them	1
14.	God will forgive us	1
15.	God will not forgive us	1
16.	(1) That God hears us	1
	(2) That we have the petitions that we desired	1
17.	By directing his prayer to God and looking up	2
18.	(1) Evening (2) Morning (3) Noon	3
19.	Always, without ceasing	1
20.	The Holy Spirit	1
21.	Enter into our closet and shut the door	1
22.	Our heavenly Father will reward us openly	1

Question	Answers	Marks
23.	Jesus Himself is in the midst	1
24.	We should agree with them concerning anything that we ask	2
25.	For kings and all in authority	1
26.	Lifting up holy hands	1
27.	(1) Wrath (2) Doubting	2
28.	Our joy is full	1

Consult Bible for written Memory Work
If word perfect, 4 marks   4
(1 mark off for each mistake. If more than 3 mistakes, no marks.)   ____

TOTAL 49

50% – 24   70% – 34   80% – 39

Notes on Correct Answers

(The numbers in the left-hand margin correspond to
the numbers of the correct answers on the previous page)

The whole Bible – and especially the New Testament – emphasizes both the willingness and the ability of God to answer prayer. (See Matt. 7:7–8.) Indeed, God is more willing to answer prayer than men are to pray. However, in order to receive the answers to our prayers, we must meet the conditions stated in God's Word. Most of the answers in this study deal with these conditions, which may be summarized as follows:

5, 8, 23. **Access only through Christ.** As sinners, we can be reconciled to God only through the propitiatory sacrifice and the mediatorial ministry of Christ. In recognition of this, we come to God through the name and the blood of Jesus.

1, 4(1), 6, 7. **Right approach**: worship, thanksgiving, praise.

1, 2, 3, 4(2), 9(1). **Right character**: truth, uprightness, righteousness, obedience (all possible only as we "abide in Christ").

8, 10(3). **Right motive:** for God's glory, not to gratify our own lusts.

10(4), 13, 14, 15, 24, 27(1). **Right relationships** with other people, especially those closest to us.

9(2), 16, 25. Praying **according to God's will**, revealed in His Word.

10(2), 12, 16(2), 27(2). **Appropriating by faith** the answer to our prayer at the actual moment that we pray. *"Now is the accepted time"* (2 Cor. 6:2).

17, 18, 19. **Regularity** and **persistence** (compare Luke 18:1).

3, 11, 21, 26. **Fervency, self-denial, commitment.**

20. In all this, we cannot rely merely upon our own will, understanding or strength, but we must have the **supernatural help of the Holy Spirit.**

22, 28. The **rewards** for right praying.

WATER BAPTISM: HOW? WHEN? WHY?

Introduction:

Jesus Himself said: *"He that believeth and is baptized shall be saved"* (Mark 16:16). God's way of salvation is still the same: first, believe; then be baptized. Believing in Christ produces an inward change in our hearts; being baptized in water is an outward act of obedience by which we testify of the change that has taken place in our hearts. By this act, we make ourselves one with Christ in His burial and in His resurrection; we are separated from the old life of sin and defeat; we come out of the water to lead a new life of righteousness and victory, made possible by God's power in us. The Scriptures in this study explain very carefully how, when and why we must be baptized.

Memory Work: Romans 6:4
Please check when memory card prepared ☐
(Review daily John 15:7)

1. What reason did Jesus Himself give for being baptized? (Matt. 3:15)

_____

_____

2. How did the Holy Spirit show that He was pleased with the baptism of Jesus? (Matt. 3:16)

_____

_____

3. What did God the Father say about Jesus when He was baptized? (Matt. 3:17)

_____

_____

4. Did Jesus go down into the water to be baptized? (Matt. 3:16)

_____

5. If a person wishes to be saved, what did Jesus say he should do after believing the gospel? (Mark 16:16)

_____

6. What did Jesus tell His disciples to do to people before baptizing them? (Matt. 28:19)

_____

7. To whom did Jesus send His disciples with this message? (Matt. 28:19)

_____

8. What does Jesus expect people to do after being baptized? (Matt. 28:20)

_____

_____

9. What did Peter tell people to do before being baptized? (Acts 2:38)

_____

10. How many people did Peter say should be baptized? (Acts 2:38)

_____

11. How did the people act who gladly received God's Word? (Acts 2:41)

_____

12. What did the people of Samaria do after they believed Philip's preaching? (Acts 8:12)

_____

13. What did Philip tell the eunuch he must do before he could be baptized? (Acts 8:37)

_____

14. What did the eunuch answer? (Acts 8:37)

_____

_____

15. Did the eunuch go down into the water to be baptized? (Acts 8:38)

_____

16. How did the eunuch feel after being baptized? (Acts 8:39)

_____

17. After Cornelius and his friends had been saved and had received the Holy Spirit, what did Peter command them to do next? (Acts 10:44–48)

_____

18. What did the Philippian jailer and his family do after believing Paul's message? (Acts 16:29–33)

_____

19. What did the disciples at Ephesus do after believing Paul's message? (Acts 19:4–5)

_____

20. Through which two experiences do believers follow Christ when they are baptized? (Rom. 6:4; Col. 2:12)

(1) _____ (2) _____

21. How does Paul say believers should live after being baptized? (Rom. 6:4)

_____

22. Is there any difference between believers of different races after being baptized? (Gal. 3:26–28)

_____

23. Mention two pictures of water baptism found in the Old Testament and referred to in the New Testament.

(1) (1 Cor. 10:1–2; Ex. 14:21–22) _____

_____

(2) (1 Pet. 3:20–21; Gen. 6 & 7) _____

_____

Memory Work: Romans 6:4

Write out this verse from memory.

_____

_____

_____

_____

DO NOT TURN THIS PAGE UNTIL YOU HAVE COMPLETED ALL ANSWERS IN THIS STUDY

STUDY NO. 9: WATER BAPTISM: HOW? WHEN? WHY?

Correct Answers and Marks

Question	Answers	Marks
1.	"Thus it becometh us to fulfil all righteousness."	1
2.	He descended like a dove and lighted upon Him	1
3.	"This is my beloved Son, in whom I am well pleased."	1
4.	Yes	1
5.	He should be baptized	1
6.	To teach them	1
7.	To all nations	1
8.	To observe all things which He has commanded	2
9.	To repent	1
10.	Every one	1
11.	They were baptized	1
12.	They were baptized	1
13.	Believe with all his heart	1
14.	"I believe that Jesus Christ is the Son of God"	1
15.	Yes	1
16.	He went on his way rejoicing	1
17.	To be baptized	1
18.	They were baptized	1
19.	They were baptized	1
20.	(1) His burial (2) His resurrection	2
21.	They should walk in newness of life	2
22.	None	1
23.	(1) The Israelites passing through the Red Sea	2
	(2) Noah and his family passing through the flood in the Ark	2

Consult Bible for written Memory Work

If word perfect, 4 marks   4

(1 mark off for each mistake. If more than 3 mistakes, no marks.)   ————

TOTAL 36

50% – 18   70% – 25   80% – 29

Notes on Correct Answers

(The numbers in the left-hand margin correspond to
the numbers of the correct answers on the previous page.)

1–4.   Although Jesus was baptized by John the Baptist, He was
not in the same class as all the others whom John baptized.
John's baptism was a *"baptism of repentance"* accompanied by
confession of sins. (See Mark 1:4–5.) But Jesus had no sins
to confess or repent of. Rather, by being baptized in this way,
Jesus set a pattern for all who would afterward follow Him in
obedience to the will of God. This is indicated by the reason
which Jesus gave: *"Thus it becometh us to fulfil all righteousness"*
(Matt. 3:15).

"*Thus*" establishes the manner of baptism: going down into,
and coming up out of, the water. "*It becometh us*" establishes a
precedent, which it becomes all sincere believers to follow. "*To
fulfil all righteousness*" establishes the reason: to complete all
righteousness. First, the Christian is made righteous through
his faith in Christ. Then, in being baptized, he completes this
inward righteousness of faith by the outward act of obedience.
Thus understood, this ordinance of baptism has the openly
expressed approval of all three Persons of the Godhead: Father,
Son and Spirit. (For a full study of this subject, see chapter 18
of Derek Prince's *The Spirit-filled Believer's Handbook*, Part III,
New Testament Baptisms.)

5, 6, 9, 13. Before being baptized, a person should fulfill the following
three conditions: (1) be taught the nature of and the reason
for the act; (2) repent of his sins; (3) believe in Jesus Christ
as the Son of God.

7, 10, 11, 12, 17, 18, 19. Jesus told His disciples that this ordinance of baptism was to be for *"all nations."* There were to be no exceptions.
In fulfillment of this, the New Testament record shows that
all new converts were always baptized without delay. In most

cases this took place on the actual day of conversion. Never was there any lengthy delay between conversion and baptism. There is no reason that this pattern should not be followed now, just as much as in the early Church.

8, 20, 21. By baptism Christians publicly identify themselves with Christ in His burial and resurrection. After baptism, they are required to lead a new life of righteousness, made possible by the grace and power of the Holy Spirit.

23(1). (1) First Cor. 10:1–2 presents a double baptism for God's people: *"in the cloud and in the sea."* Baptism *"in the cloud"* typifies baptism in the Holy Spirit. Baptism *"in the sea"* typifies water baptism.

23(2). (2) By faith Noah and his family entered into the Ark (= Christ). Then, in the Ark, they passed through the water of the flood (= baptism). They were thus saved from God's judgment; separated from the old, ungodly world; and ushered into a completely new life.

WITNESSING AND WINNING SOULS

Introduction:

By His atoning death on the cross, Christ has made salvation possible for all men everywhere. But in order to receive salvation each person must first hear the Word of God and the testimony of Christ. God's plan is that every person who is saved should be filled with the Holy Spirit and should then use this power to witness to others of Christ, and that in this way the testimony of Christ should continually be extended farther and farther abroad, until it has reached the uttermost part of the earth and until nations have heard. This is the great way in which all Christians can work together to prepare the way for the return of Christ. Christians who are faithful in witnessing will receive a reward from Christ Himself, and will have the joy of seeing in heaven the souls who have been won through their testimony. Christians who are unfaithful will have to answer to God for lost souls to whom they failed to witness.

Memory Work: Acts 1:8
Please check when memory card prepared ☐
(Review daily Romans 6:4)

1. What did Christ tell His disciples that they were to be for Him? (Acts 1:8)

   _____

2. How far did Christ say that the witness of His disciples was to extend? (Acts 1:8)

   _____

3. To whom must the witness be extended before the end of this age? (Matt. 24:14)

   _____

4. Of what three things concerning Jesus did Peter say that he and the other disciples were witnesses? (Acts 10:39–41)

   (1) _____

   (2) _____ (3) _____

5. What did God tell Paul that he was to do for Christ? (Acts 22:15)

   _____

   _____

6. What did Paul continue to do from the day that he came to know Jesus? (Acts 26:22)

   _____

   _____

7. What does a true witness do by his testimony? (Prov. 14:25)

   _____

8. What should a wise Christian seek to do? (Prov. 11:30)

   _____

9. After Andrew found Jesus, whom did he in turn bring to Jesus? (John 1:35–42)

_____

10. After Jesus found Philip, whom did Philip in turn bring to Jesus? (John 1:43–47)

_____

11. When the Pharisees questioned the man born blind, what did he answer from his own experience? (John 9:25)

_____

12. What two things should we talk about and make known to other people? (1 Chron. 16:8–9)

(1) _____ (2) _____

13. When people opposed Paul's testimony in Corinth, what did God tell Paul? (Acts 18:9)

_____

14. What spirit did Paul tell Timothy was not from God? (2 Tim. 1:7)

_____

15. What does the fear of man bring? (Prov. 29:25)

_____

16. What instruction did Paul give Timothy concerning the testimony of Christ? (2 Tim. 1:8)

_____

17. When Peter and John were commanded not to speak about Jesus, what two answers did they give?

    (1) (Acts 4:20) _____

    (2) (Acts 5:29) _____

18. When the other disciples heard that Peter and John had been forbidden to speak about Jesus, what did they all do? (Acts 4:24)

    _____

19. After the disciples had prayed and been filled with the Holy Ghost, what did they all do? (Acts 4:31)

    _____

20. What special position did God give Ezekiel among his people? (Ezek. 3:17)

    _____

21. What did God tell Ezekiel would happen to him if he failed to warn the sinners? (Ezek. 3:18)

    _____

22. What two things did Paul testify to all men at Ephesus? (Acts 20:21)

    (1) _____

    (2) _____

23. Why could Paul say he was pure from the blood of all men at Ephesus? (Acts 20:26–27)

    _____

24. What is the final reward laid up for all faithful witnesses of Christ? (2 Tim. 4:8)

_____

Memory Work: Acts 1:8

Write out this verse from memory.

_____

_____

_____

DO NOT TURN THIS PAGE UNTIL YOU HAVE COMPLETED ALL ANSWERS IN THIS STUDY

STUDY NO. 10: WITNESSING AND WINNING SOULS

Correct Answers and Marks

Question	Answers	Marks
1.	Witnesses	1
2.	To the uttermost part of the earth	1
3.	To all nations	1
4.	(1) All that He did (2) His death (3) His resurrection	3
5.	To be His witness to all men of what he had seen and heard	3
6.	Witnessing both to small and great that the Scriptures were true	3
7.	He delivers souls	1
8.	To win souls	1
9.	His brother, Simon Peter	1
10.	Nathanael	1
11.	*"One thing I know, that, whereas I was blind, now I see."*	2
12.	(1) God's deeds (2) His wondrous works	2
13.	"Be not afraid, but speak…"	2
14.	The spirit of fear	1
15.	A snare	1
16.	Not to be ashamed of the testimony of Christ	2
17.	(1) *"We cannot but speak the things which we have seen and heard."*	2
	(2) *"We ought to obey God rather than men."*	1
18.	They all prayed to God with one accord	2
19.	They spoke the word of God with boldness	1
20.	A watchman	1
21.	God would require their blood at his hand	2
22.	(1) Repentance toward God	1
	(2) Faith toward our Lord Jesus Christ	1
23.	Because he had not shunned to declare unto them all the counsel of God	2
24.	A crown of righteousness	1

Consult Bible for written Memory Work
If word perfect, 4 marks   4
(1 mark off for each mistake. If more than 3 mistakes, no marks.)   ____

                                                              TOTAL 44

      50% – 22   70% – 31   80% – 35

Notes on Correct Answers

(The numbers in the left-hand margin correspond to
the numbers of the correct answers on the previous page.)

1.   Christians are not intended to be witnesses primarily to a doctrine, an experience, or a denomination, but to **Christ Himself.** Jesus said, *"I, if I be lifted up from the earth, will draw all men unto me"* (John 12:32). Christian testimony should uplift Jesus. To do this effectively, it must be directed and empowered by the Holy Spirit.

4.   Compare Acts 1:21–22 and 4:33. The central fact of all testimony concerning Christ is His **resurrection** from the dead.

5–6.   Paul's testimony is a pattern for all Christians. It was based on personal experience; it pointed to Christ; it confirmed the record of the Scriptures.

7–8.   Faithful personal testimony is the most effective way to win other souls to Christ.

9–10.   Although Peter later became the acknowledged leader among the apostles and the chief preacher, it was his brother Andrew who first came to Christ and then brought Peter in turn. Later, Philip in the same way brought Nathanael. Thus the pattern of individual soul-winning is set by the apostles themselves.

11.   Someone has said: "The man with an experience is not at the mercy of the man with an argument."

12.   A Christian's conversation should be positive, glorifying God, and building his own faith and that of others.

13–16, 19. The greatest hindrance to effective testimony is *"the spirit of fear"* (timidity). The Bible teaches clearly that this spirit does not come from God and that a Christian should not allow himself to be ensnared or bound by it. The remedy is to be filled with the Holy Spirit.

17(2). Where there is a clear-cut choice between obedience to God and obedience to man, this answer of Peter and John is just as valid today.

18. Prayer is the great weapon given to Christians to break down the barriers to their testimony.

20–23. Like Ezekiel in the Old Testament, Paul in the New Testament understood that he would be held accountable by God for those to whom he had been given opportunity to testify. He understood also that he was required by God to *"keep back nothing,"* but to declare *"all the counsel of God."* God still requires the same of Christians today.

GOD'S PLAN FOR PROSPERITY

Introduction:

All through the Bible God promises to bless and prosper those who trust and serve Him. In order to receive God's financial and material blessings, we must learn to follow God's rule of faith, which says, "*Give, and it shall be given unto you*" (Luke 6:38). We begin by giving back to God the first tenth of all that we receive, in money or in produce. This first tenth, set aside for God, is called our *tithe*. Over and above this "tithe," we bring our *offerings* to God, as the Holy Spirit directs us. As we do this in faith, God abundantly blesses us and supplies all our needs.

Memory Work: Matt. 6:33
Please check when memory card prepared ☐
(Review daily Acts 1:8)

A. Examples of God's Servants Who Have Prospered

1. When God gave Abraham victory in battle, what did Abraham give back to God's priest, Melchizedek? (Gen. 14:19–20)

   _____

2. How did God in turn deal with Abraham? (Gen. 24:1)

_____

3. What three things did Jacob want God to do for him? (Gen. 28:20)

(1) _____

(2) _____

(3) _____

4. What did Jacob promise to give God in return? (Gen. 28:22)

_____

5. How did God in turn deal with Jacob? (Gen. 33:11)

_____

6. What kind of man was Joseph? (Gen. 39:2)

_____

7. What was the reason for Joseph's prosperity? (Gen. 39:2, 23)

_____

8. What three things did God command Joshua concerning His law? (Josh. 1:8)

(1) _____

(2) _____

(3) _____

9. What did God promise Joshua if he would do these three things? (Josh. 1:8)

_____

10. What did David promise Solomon if he would obey all the statutes and judgments of God's law? (1 Chron. 22:13)

_____

11. As long as Uzziah sought the Lord, what did God do for him? (2 Chron. 26:5)

_____

12. When Hezekiah sought and served God with all his heart, what happened to him? (2 Chron. 31:21; 32:30)

_____

B. Conditions and Promises of Prosperity

13. Concerning a certain kind of person, God says that _"whatever he doeth shall prosper"_ (Ps. 1:3).

(a) Write down three things that such a person _must not_ do. (Ps. 1:1)

(1) _____

(2) _____

(3) _____

(b) Write down two things that such a person _must_ do. (Ps. 1:2)

(1) _____

(2) _____

14. In what two ways did God say that Israel had been robbing Him? (Mal. 3:8)

(1) _____ (2) _____

15. What happened to Israel as a result of robbing God? (Mal 3:9)

_____

16. How did God tell Israel to "prove" Him (i.e. put Him to the test)? (Mal. 3:10)

_____

17. What did God promise Israel that He would then do for them? (Mal. 3:10)

_____

_____

18. What two things does Christ tell Christians to seek before all others? (Matt. 6:33)

(1) _____ (2) _____

19. What result does Christ promise will then follow? (Matt. 6:33)

_____

20. When we give, with what measure will it be given back to us? (Luke 6:38)

_____

21. By what standard did Paul tell each Christian to measure how much he should set aside for God? (1 Cor. 16:2)

_____

22. For what purpose did Christ become poor? (2 Cor. 8:9)

_____

23. What kind of person does God love? (2 Cor. 9:7)

_____

24. If we wish to reap bountifully, what must we do first? (2 Cor. 9:6)

_____

25. If God's grace abounds towards us, what two results will follow? (2 Cor. 9:8)

(1) _____

(2) _____

26. From what kind of people will God withhold no good thing? (Ps. 84:11)

_____

27. What kind of people will not want (lack) any good thing? (Ps. 34:10)

_____

28. In what does the Lord take pleasure? (Ps. 35:27)

_____

Memory Work: Matthew 6:33
Write out this verse from memory.

_____

_____

_____

DO NOT TURN THIS PAGE UNTIL YOU HAVE COMPLETED ALL ANSWERS IN THIS STUDY

STUDY NO. 11:
GOD'S PLAN FOR PROSPERITY

Correct Answers and Marks

Question	Answers	Marks
1.	Tithes of all	1
2.	God blessed Abraham in all things	1
3.	(1) Be with him (2) Keep him in the way that he went	2
	(3) Give him bread to eat and raiment to put on	1
4.	A tenth of all that God would give him	1
5.	God dealt graciously with Jacob	1
6.	A prosperous man	1
7.	The Lord was with him and made what he did to prosper	1
8.	(1) It should not depart from his mouth	1
	(2) He should meditate in it day and night	1
	(3) He should observe to do everything that was written in it	1
9.	He would make his way prosperous and he would have good success	2
10.	Then shalt thou prosper	1
11.	God made him to prosper	1
12.	He prospered in all his works	1
13.	(a) (1) NOT walk in the counsel of the ungodly	1
	(2) NOT stand in the path of sinners	1
	(3) NOT sit in the seat of the scornful	1
	(b) (1) He MUST delight in the law of the Lord	1
	(2) He MUST meditate in it day and night	1
14.	(1) In tithes (2) In offerings	2
15.	The whole nation was cursed with a curse	1
16.	By bringing all the tithes into the storehouse	1
17.	Open the windows of heaven and pour out such a blessing that there would not be room to contain it	2
18.	(1) The kingdom of God (2) The righteousness of God	2

Question	Answers	Marks
19.	All the material things that they need will be added to them	1
20.	With the same measure that we "mete" (= measure) with	1
21.	As God hath prospered him	1
22.	That we through His poverty might be rich	2
23.	A cheerful giver	1
24.	We must sow bountifully	1
25.	(1) We shall always have all sufficiency in all things	1
	(2) We shall abound to every good work	1
26.	Them that walk uprightly	1
27.	They that seek the Lord	1
28.	In the prosperity of His servant	1

Consult Bible for written Memory Work
If word perfect, 4 marks   4
(1 mark off for each mistake. If more than 3 mistakes in either verse,
no marks for that verse.)
                                                                                      ____
                                                                          TOTAL 46

50% – 23   70% – 32   80% – 37

Notes on Correct Answers

(The numbers in the left-hand margin correspond to
the numbers of the correct answers on the previous page.)

1–5.   Note that the practice of "tithing" did not begin with the law of
Moses. The first person recorded in the Bible as giving tithes is
Abraham. In Rom. 4:11–12, Abraham is called *"the father of all
them that believe … who also walk in the steps of that faith of our
father Abraham."* Believers who give their tithes to God today
are certainly "walking in the steps of the faith of Abraham."
Note also that the priest to whom Abraham gave tithes was
Melchizedek. In Hebrews 5, 6, and 7, it is shown that Christ

is our great *"High Priest after the order of Melchizedek."* In this capacity, He still receives the tithes of His believing people.

Both Abraham and Jacob experienced God's material blessings as a result of their tithing. In Gen. 32:10, Jacob says, *"With my staff I passed over Jordan, and now I am become two bands."* When Jacob started to give tithes to God, he owned nothing but the staff in his hand. Twenty years later he was the prosperous head of a large and flourishing household.

6–7.   Outward circumstances cannot prevent God from keeping His promises. Even in the prison Joseph prospered. Much more so, when he became prime minister of Egypt. Joseph's prosperity was the outworking of his character and his relationship to God.

8–9.   Joshua was called to lead God's people into "the Promised Land." Today Christians are called to enter "a land of promises." Then or now, the conditions for success are the same. Note especially the importance of right meditation. Compare the answer to question 13b2.

10–12. From David to the Babylonian captivity, God prospered every king of Judah who was obedient to the law and faithful in the service of the temple.

13.   Note that Ps. 1:1–3 does not describe one particular historical character but applies generally to every believer who fulfills the conditions stated.

14–15. Unfaithfulness by God's people in giving to God can bring a national curse. This principle still applies today.

16–21. The only basis of righteousness acceptable to God is *faith*. *"Whatsoever is not of faith is sin"* (Rom. 14:23). (Compare Heb. 11:6.) This principle applies in our financial dealings as much as in every other part of our life.

22.   According to the Bible, poverty is a curse. Deut. 28:15–68 lists all the curses that result from breaking God's law. In verse 48 the following are included: *"Thou shalt serve thine enemies . . . in*

hunger…in thirst…in nakedness…in want of all things." This is absolute poverty. On the cross Christ took upon Himself every one of these curses. (See Gal. 3:13–14.) He was hungry, thirsty, naked, in want of all things. He did this that believers might in return receive God's abundant provision for every need. (See Phil. 4:19.)

23. *"Cheerful"*; literally, "hilarious."

24. Christians should give in the same way that a farmer sows seed – carefully, intelligently, in the area calculated to yield the best returns for God's kingdom.

26–28. Prosperity is God's will for His believing, obedient people.

THE SECOND COMING OF CHRIST

Introduction:

When Jesus Christ first came to earth 2,000 years ago, His coming exactly fulfilled in every detail all the prophecies of the Bible relating to that event. When He left this earth to return to heaven, He promised His disciples very definitely that He would come back to the earth again. Apart from these promises which Jesus Himself gave, there are many prophecies throughout the whole Bible concerning the second coming of Christ – even more, in fact, than there are about His first coming. Since the prophecies of His first coming were exactly and literally fulfilled, it is reasonable to believe that the prophecies of His second coming will be fulfilled in the same way. The Scriptures in this study contain the clear promises of Christ's return. They also tell us what will happen to Christians at that time, and how Christians must in the meanwhile prepare themselves.

Memory Work: Luke 21:36
Please check when memory card prepared ☐
(Review daily Matt. 6:33)

A. Promises of Christ's Return

1. For what purpose did Christ say He was leaving His disciples? (John 14:2)

   _____

2. What promise did Christ give His disciples when He left them? (John 14:3)

   _____

3. When Christ was taken up into heaven, what promise did the angels give? (Acts 1:11)

   _____

   _____

4. What is the _"blessed hope"_ to which all true Christians look forward? (Tit. 2:13)

   _____

5. What three sounds will be heard when Christ descends from heaven? (1 Thess. 4:16)

   (1) _____ (2) _____

   (3) _____

B. What Will Happen to Christians

6. Will all Christians have died when Messiah comes? (1 Cor. 15:51)

   _____

7. At this time what will happen to Christians who have died? (1 Thess. 4:16)

_____

8. Write down two things that will then happen to all Christians, whether they have died or not.

(1) (1 Cor. 15:51) _____

_____

(2) (1 Thess. 4:17) _____

_____

9. Will these Christians ever again be separated from the Lord? (1 Thess. 4:17)

_____

10. When we actually see the Lord, what change will take place in us? (1 John 3:2)

_____

11. As a result of this change, what will the body of the Christian then be like? (Phil. 3:21)

_____

12. What two words does Paul use to describe the body of the Christian after resurrection? (1 Cor. 15:53)

(1) _____ (2) _____

13. How does the Bible describe the feast which Christians will then enjoy? (Rev. 19:9)

_____

C. How Christians Must Prepare

14. What did the Lamb's wife do before the marriage supper? (Rev. 19:7)

_____

15. What kind of clothing did she wear? (Rev. 19:8)

_____

16. What does the fine linen represent? (Rev. 19:8)

_____

17. Of the ten virgins, which ones went in to the marriage? (Matt. 25:10)

_____

18. If a man has the hope of seeing the Lord when He comes, how does he prepare himself for this? (1 John 3:3)

_____

19. To whom will Christ appear the second time unto salvation? (Heb. 9:28)

_____

20. What two things must we follow after, if we desire to see the Lord? (Heb. 12:14)

(1) _____ (2) _____

21. Write down three conditions which should mark out all Christians at Christ's coming. (2 Pet. 3:14)

(1) _____ (2) _____ (3) _____

22. What expression does Christ use to show how sudden His coming will be? (Rev. 3:3; 16:15)

_____

23. Who knows the day and hour of Christ's coming? (Mark 13:32)

_____

24. What did Christ warn all Christians to do in view of His coming? (Mark 13:35–37)

_____

25. What did Christ warn Christians to do in addition to watching? (Luke 21:36)

_____

26. What three things did Christ warn Christians could keep them from being ready? (Luke 21:34)

(1) _____ (2) _____ (3) _____

Memory Work: Luke 21:36
Write out this verse from memory.

_____

_____

_____

DO NOT TURN THIS PAGE UNTIL YOU HAVE COMPLETED ALL ANSWERS IN THIS STUDY

STUDY NO. 12: THE SECOND COMING OF CHRIST

Correct Answers and Marks

Question	Answers	Marks
1.	To go and prepare a place for them	1
2.	"I will come again and receive you unto Myself"	2
3.	This same Jesus shall so come in like manner as ye have seen Him go into heaven	2
4.	The glorious appearing of the great God and our Saviour Jesus Christ	2
5.	(1) A shout (2) The voice of the archangel	2
	(3) The trump of God	1
6.	No	1
7.	They will arise (from the dead)	1
8.	(1) They will all be changed	1
	(2) They will all be caught up in the clouds to meet the Lord in the air	2
9.	Never	1
10.	We shall be like Him	1
11.	Like the glorious (glorified) body of Christ	1
12.	(1) Incorruption (2) Immortality	2
13.	The marriage supper of the Lamb (Christ)	1
14.	She made herself ready	1
15.	Fine linen, clean and white (bright)	1
16.	The righteousness of saints	1
17.	They that were ready	1
18.	He purifies himself even as He (Christ) is pure	2
19.	To them that look for Him	1
20.	(1) Peace with all men (2) Holiness	2
21.	(1) In peace (2) Without spot (3) Blameless	3
22.	"As a thief"	1
23.	Only God the Father	1
24.	To watch	1

Question	Answers	Marks
25.	To pray always	1
26.	(1) Surfeiting (gluttony) (2) Drunkenness (3) Cares of this life	3

Consult Bible for written Memory Work
If word perfect, 4 marks   4
(1 mark off for each mistake. If more than 3 mistakes in either verse,
no marks for that verse.)
                                                                              ——
                                                                     TOTAL 44

50% – 22   70% – 31   80% – 35

Notes on Correct Answers

(The numbers in the left-hand margin correspond to
the numbers of the correct answers on the previous page.)

1–5.   *"Out of the mouth of two or three witnesses shall every word be established"* (Matt. 18:16, etc.). Concerning the return of Christ we have the three witnesses: (1) Christ Himself (John 14:3); (2) the angels (Acts 1:11); (3) the apostle Paul (1 Thess. 4:16). Note the emphasis on the return of Christ *in person: "This same Jesus…"; "The Lord Himself…"* This *"blessed hope"* is the supreme goal of all Christian living.

5.   (1) The *"shout"* will come from the Lord Himself, for His voice alone has power to call forth the dead. (See John 5:28–29.) (2) The archangel will presumably be Gabriel, whose special duty is to announce impending interventions of God in the affairs of men. (See Luke 1:19, 26.) (3) The trumpet is used to call God's people together. (See Num. 10:2–3.)

6.   To *"sleep"* means to die (compare Acts 7:60; 1 Cor. 11:30). This word is particularly used of the death of Christians because they look forward to "waking" again on the resurrection morning.

6–8.   The following order of events is indicated: (1) Dead Christians will be resurrected with new, glorified bodies. (2) Living Christians will have their bodies instantaneously changed to similar, glorified bodies. (3) All Christians will be caught up together in the clouds to meet the Lord as He descends from heaven.

10–12. The glorified body of the Christian will be like the Lord's own glorified body. (For a fuller study of this subject, see Derek Prince's book *Foundational Truths for Christian Living*, Part VI, Resurrection of the Dead.)

13.   Compare Matt. 8:11, 26:29.

14–21, 24–25. The Bible very clearly teaches that, in order to be ready for the return of Christ, Christians will have to prepare themselves diligently. In Rev. 19:8, the literal translation is "the righteousnesses – or righteous acts – of saints." This is the outworking in practical Christian living of the righteousness of Christ received by faith. (Compare Phil. 2:12–13: "*Work out… for it is God that worketh in you.*") The main requirements of God's Word in this respect may be summarized as follows (1) Purity (without spot) (1 John 3:3; 2 Pet. 3:14); (2) Holiness (Heb. 12:14); (3) Peace (= right relations with all men) (Heb. 12:14; 2 Pet. 3:14); (4) Blamelessness (= faithfulness in all Christian duties) (2 Pet. 3:14); (5) Expectancy (Heb. 9:28); (6) Watchfulness (Mark 13:37); (7) Prayerfulness (Luke 21:36).

22.   Christ will be "*like a thief*" in the manner of His coming, but He will take only that which is His own. It is "*they that are Christ's at His coming*" (1 Cor. 15:23).

23.   When the moment comes, the Father will tell the Son. Then all heaven will be stirred to action.

26.   (1) Christ always warned against "gluttony" *before* "drunkenness."

        (3) Compare Luke 17:27–28. The things mentioned here are not sinful in themselves. The sin consists in becoming absorbed in them.

SIGNS OF CHRIST'S COMING

Introduction:

The Bible tells us of various special things which will be happening in the world at the time just before Christ's second coming, and which will be signs to warn us that He is coming soon. In this study some of the most important signs are stated. They are divided into two groups: **A. Signs in the World of Religion**; and **B. Signs in the World at Large**. Below each group of signs are given the references to the passages of Scripture in which those signs are mentioned.

In this study you are required to do the following:

1. Read through the signs in Group A.
2. Read through the Scriptures of which the references are given below Group A.
3. On the line below each sign, write in the reference of the Scripture which mentions that sign.
4. Repeat the same procedure for Group B.
5. At the end of each sign, you will see a square box ☐. When you have done the rest of the study, read through the signs once again, and check each box if you feel that that particular sign is being fulfilled in the world as you know it today.

(NOTE: There is one appropriate Scripture reference for each sign.

However, Matt. 24:7 applies to three different signs, and must be written in after each sign to which it applies.)

Memory Work: Luke 21:28
Please check when memory card prepared ☐
(Review daily Luke 21:36)

A. Signs in the World of Religion

1. Worldwide outpouring of the Holy Spirit ☐

   _____

2. Worldwide evangelism and missionary activity ☐

   _____

3. Christians afflicted, killed and hated ☐

   _____

4. Many false prophets ☐

   _____

5. A great falling away from the Christian faith ☐

   _____

6. Many Christians being led astray by deceptions of the devil ☐

   _____

7. The love of many Christians growing cold ☐

   _____

Scripture References:

Matthew 24:12	1 Timothy 4:1	Matthew 24:9	Acts 2:17
Matthew 24:11	2 Thess. 2:3	Matthew 24:14	

B. Signs in the World at Large

8. Great international wars ☐

---

9. Increase of travel and knowledge ☐

---

10. Rise of Zionism and rebuilding of the State of Israel ☐

---

11. Jerusalem liberated from Gentile dominion ☐

---

12. Many scoffers, denying the Word of God and the promise of Christ's return ☐

---

13. People absorbed in material pleasures and pursuits, and forgetting the impending judgments of God ☐

---

14. Great decline in moral and ethical standards, combined with the outward forms of religion ☐

---

15. Abounding iniquity (literally, "lawlessness") ☐

---

16. Famines and pestilences ☐

---

17. Increase in severity and frequency of earthquakes ☐

---

18. Distress and perplexity of nations ☐

_____

19. Many antichrists ☐

_____

Scripture References:

Matthew 24:12	Luke 21:24	1 John 2:18	2 Peter 3:2–7
Daniel 12:4	Matthew 24:7	Luke 17:26–30	Ps. 102:16
2 Tim. 3:1–5	Luke 21:25		

Memory Work: Luke 21:28
Write out this verse from memory.

_____

_____

_____

DO NOT TURN THIS PAGE UNTIL YOU HAVE COMPLETED ALL ANSWERS IN THIS STUDY

Three Final Important Questions

There are nineteen different signs of Christ's coming mentioned in this study.

1. Against how many of them did you place a check?

   _____

2. Does this indicate to you that Christ may be coming soon?

   _____

3. If so, are you *ready*?

   _____

STUDY NO. 13: SIGNS OF CHRIST'S COMING

Correct Answers and Marks

Question No.	Answers	Marks
1.	Acts 2:17	1
2.	Matthew 24:14	1
3.	Matthew 24:9	1
4.	Matthew 24:11	1
5.	2 Thessalonians 2:3	1
6.	1 Timothy 4:1	1
7.	Matthew 24:12	1
8.	Matthew 24:7	1
9.	Daniel 12:4	1
10.	Psalm 102:16	1
11.	Luke 21:24	1
12.	2 Peter 3:2–7	1
13.	Luke 17:26–30	1
14.	2 Timothy 3:1–5	1
15.	Matthew 24:12	1
16.	Matthew 24:7	1
17.	Matthew 24:7	1
18.	Luke 21:25	1
19.	1 John 2:18	1

Consult Bible for written Memory Work
If word perfect, 4 marks   4
(1 mark off for each mistake. If more than 3 mistakes in either verse,
no marks for that verse.)
                                                                                        ____
                                                                        TOTAL 23

50% – 11   70% – 16   80% – 18

Notes on Correct Answers

(The numbers in the left-hand margin correspond to
the numbers of the correct answers on the previous page.)

1.   The expression *"all flesh"* denotes the entire human race. It is
     often used with this meaning in the prophets. (See Is. 40:5–6;
     Jer. 25:31; Ezek. 21:4–5.) Every section of the human race will
     feel the impact of this last great outpouring of God's Spirit.

2.   Evangelistic and missionary outreach are the natural outcome
     of the outpouring of God's Spirit. Note the special comment
     after this sign: *"And then shall the end come."*

3.   It is estimated that there have been more Christian martyrs
     in this century than in any preceding century. Under atheistic
     communism, amongst one-third of the world's population,
     Christianity is systematically persecuted.

4–6. These three signs all indicate a tremendous increase towards
     the close of this age in satanic pressures and deceptions aimed
     at seducing Christians from their loyalty to Christ. The Bible
     indicates that at the end there will be only two significant
     groups within Christendom, the one described as a *"bride,"*
     and the other as a *"harlot."* The *"bride"* is identified by her
     faithfulness to the *"bridegroom"* (= Christ). Conversely, the
     "harlot" is identified by her unfaithfulness to Christ. (See Rev.
     17 and 18.)

7.   This sign corresponds with the picture of Laodicea, the last
     of the seven churches of Revelation, whose damning sin is
     "lukewarmness" (Rev. 3:14–22). This decline in the love of
     Christians will be mainly due to one or more of the follow-
     ing factors: (1) bitter persecution; (2) satanic deception; (3)
     prevailing materialism.

8.   This century has seen wars greater and more numerous than
     any preceding century, especially the two "World Wars."

9.   Note how these two factors are logically connected. The

increase in knowledge (science) has made possible the increase in travel. Likewise, the increase in travel contributes to the increase of knowledge.

10–11. The rise of Zionism, the rebirth of the State of Israel, and the Six-day War of 1967 are among the great miracles of modern history. Someone has said: "The Jews are the minute hand on God's prophetic clock, and that hand has almost reached midnight."

12. The past century has witnessed systematic attacks on the Bible such as no previous century can record. Paradoxically enough, these attacks on the Bible are actually confirmations of its accuracy since the Bible clearly predicts them.

13–15, 18. These signs are attested daily by the newspapers of the modern world. (Compare Luke 17:26 with Gen. 6:5, 12–13.) The three main evil features of Noah's day were: (1) evil imaginations; (2) sexual corruption and perversion; (3) violence.

16. Famines and pestilences naturally tend to go together, and both are often caused by war.

17. Records over the past century indicate a marked increase in the frequency of earthquakes.

19. The work of *"the spirit of antichrist"* is twofold: first, to displace Christ from His God-given position of authority and supremacy; second, to raise up another in Christ's place. In this sense, the three main political "isms" of this generation – Facism, Nazism and Communism – have all been "anti-Christian" (as are many other political and religious forces at work in the world today). However, the world still awaits the final "antichrist," as described in 2 Thess. 2:3–12, etc.

REVIEW

Introduction:

The purpose of this last study is to fix firmly in your mind the many important truths which you have learned from the previous studies. Review is an essential part of all thorough learning. If you are willing to work steadily through this last study, carefully following the instructions step by step, you will greatly increase the benefit and blessing which you have received from the previous studies, and you will find out for yourself just how much you have really learned. Do not omit the review of the memory work!

Final Memory Work: James 1:25
Please check when memory card prepared ☐
(Review daily Luke 21:28)

First, read carefully through all the questions of the previous thirteen studies, together with the corresponding correct answers. Check that you now know and understand the correct answer to each question.

Second, review all the passages which you have learned for Memory work.

Third, write the answers to Sections A and B below.

Section A:

Write below, in the spaces provided, four important truths from the Bible which you have learned from this course. In each case, write down the references to the passages in the Bible where that truth is found.

First truth _____

_____

_____

_____

_____

Bible references _____

_____

Second truth _____

_____

_____

_____

_____

Bible references _____

_____

Third truth _____

_____

_____

_____

_____

Bible references _____
_____

Fourth truth _____
_____
_____
_____

Bible references _____
_____

Section B:

In the space below, describe briefly any important changes which have taken place in your own life through studying the Bible.

_____
_____
_____
_____
_____
_____
_____

NOTE: There are no marks allotted for Sections A and B above.

Final Memory Work: James 1:25
Write out this verse from memory.

_____

_____

_____

Marks for the above Memory Work:

If word perfect, 4 marks for each verse   4

(1 mark off for each mistake. If more than 3 mistakes, no marks.)   ____

TOTAL 4

MARKS FOR THE COURSE

How to assess your own results:

Write your marks for each study in the space provided below in the right-hand column. Add up your own total and compare it with the standards given for Pass, Credit, or Distinction.

STUDY NO. 1	54	_____
STUDY NO. 2	40	_____
STUDY NO. 3	40	_____
STUDY NO. 4	44	_____
STUDY NO. 5	49	_____
STUDY NO. 6	38	_____
STUDY NO. 7	59	_____
STUDY NO. 8	49	_____
STUDY NO. 9	36	_____
STUDY NO. 10	44	_____
STUDY NO. 11	46	_____
STUDY NO. 12	44	_____
STUDY NO. 13	23	_____
STUDY NO. 14	4	_____
TOTAL	570 TOTAL	
PASS	50% and over	285
CREDIT	70% and over	399
DISTINCTION	80% and over	456

CONGRATULATIONS ON COMPLETING THE COURSE!

ABOUT THE AUTHOR

*D*erek Prince (1915–2003) was born in India of British parents. He was educated as a scholar of Greek and Latin at Eton College and King's College, Cambridge in England. Upon graduation he held a fellowship (equivalent to a professorship) in Ancient and Modern Philosophy at King's College. Prince also studied Hebrew, Aramaic, and modern languages at Cambridge and the Hebrew University in Jerusalem. As a student, he was a philosopher and self-proclaimed agnostic.

Bible Teacher

While in the British Medical Corps during World War II, Prince began to study the Bible as a philosophical work. Converted through a powerful encounter with Jesus Christ, he was baptized in the Holy Spirit a few days later. Out of this encounter, he formed two conclusions: first, that Jesus Christ is alive; second, that the Bible is a true, relevant, up-to-date book. These conclusions altered the whole course of his life, which he then devoted to studying and teaching the Bible as the Word of God.

Discharged from the army in Jerusalem in 1945, he married Lydia Christensen, founder of a children's home there. Upon their marriage, he immediately became father to Lydia's eight adopted daughters – six Jewish, one Palestinian Arab, and one English. Together, the family saw the rebirth of the state of Israel in 1948. In the late 1950s, they adopted another daughter while Prince was serving as principal of a teacher training college in Kenya.

In 1963, the Princes immigrated to the United States and pastored a church in Seattle. In 1973, Prince became one of the founders of Intercessors for America. His book *Shaping History through Prayer and Fasting* has awakened Christians around the world to their responsibility to pray for their governments. Many consider underground translations of the book as instrumental in the fall of communist regimes in the USSR, East Germany, and Czechoslovakia.

Lydia Prince died in 1975, and Prince married Ruth Baker (a single mother to three adopted children) in 1978. He met his second wife, like his first wife, while she was serving the Lord in Jerusalem. Ruth died in December 1998 in Jerusalem, where they had lived since 1981.

Teaching, Preaching and Broadcasting

Until a few years before his own death in 2003 at the age of eighty-eight, Prince persisted in the ministry God had called him to as he traveled the world, imparting God's revealed truth, praying for the sick and afflicted, and sharing his prophetic insights into world events in the light of Scripture. Internationally recognized as a Bible scholar and spiritual patriarch, Derek Prince established a teaching ministry that spanned six continents and more than sixty years. He is the author of more than fifty books, six hundred audio teachings, and one hundred video teachings, many of which have been translated and published in more than one hundred languages. He pioneered teaching on such groundbreaking themes as generational curses, the biblical significance of Israel, and demonology.

Prince's radio program, which began in 1979, has been translated into more than a dozen languages and continues to touch lives. Derek's main gift of explaining the Bible and its teaching in a clear and simple way has helped build a foundation of faith in millions of lives. His nondenominational, nonsectarian approach has made his teaching equally relevant and helpful to people from all racial and religious backgrounds, and his teaching is estimated to have reached more than half the globe.

DPM Worldwide Ministry

In 2002, he said, "It is my desire – and I believe the Lord's desire – that this ministry continue the work, which God began through me over sixty years ago, until Jesus returns."

Derek Prince Ministries International continues to reach out to believers in over 140 countries with Derek's teaching, fulfilling the mandate to keep on "until Jesus returns." This is accomplished through the outreaches of more than thirty Derek Prince offices around the world, including primary work in Australia, Canada, China, France, Germany, the Netherlands, New Zealand, Norway, Russia, South Africa, Switzerland, the United Kingdom, and the United States. For current information about these and other world-wide locations, visit www.derekprince.com.

READ THROUGH THE BIBLE IN ONE YEAR

Day 1: Genesis 1–2; Matthew 1

Day 2: Genesis 3–5; Matthew 2

Day 3: Genesis 6–8; Matthew 3

Day 4: Genesis 9–11; Matthew 4

Day 5: Genesis 12–14; Matthew 5:1–26

Day 6: Genesis 15–17; Matthew 5:27–48

Day 7: Genesis 18–19; Matthew 6

Day 8: Genesis 20–22; Matthew 7

Day 9: Genesis 23–24; Matthew 8

Day 10: Genesis 25–26; Matthew 9:1–17

Day 11: Genesis 27–28; Matthew 9:18–38

Day 12: Genesis 29–30; Matthew 10:1–23

Day 13: Genesis 31–32; Matthew 10:24–42

Day 14: Genesis 33–35; Matthew 11

Day 15: Genesis 36–37; Matthew 12:1–21

Day 16: Genesis 38–40; Matthew 12:22–50

Day 17: Genesis 41; Matthew 13:1–32

Day 18: Genesis 42–43; Matthew 13:33–58

Day 19: Genesis 44–45; Matthew 14:1–21

Day 20: Genesis 46–48; Matthew 14:22–36

Day 21: Genesis 49–50; Matthew 15:1–20

Day 22: Exodus 1–3; Matthew 15:21–39

Day 23: Exodus 4–6; Matthew 16

Day 24: Exodus 7–8; Matthew 17

Day 25: Exodus 9–10; Matthew 18:1–20

Day 26: Exodus 11–12; Matthew 18:21–35

Day 27: Exodus 13–15; Matthew 19:1–15

Day 28: Exodus 16–18; Matthew 19:16–30

Day 29: Exodus 19–21; Matthew 20:1–16

Day 30: Exodus 22–23; Matthew 20:17–34

Day 31: Exodus 24–26; Matthew 21:1–22

Day 32: Exodus 27–28; Matthew 21:23–46

Day 33: Exodus 29–30; Matthew 22:1–22

Day 34: Exodus 31–33; Matthew 22:23–46

Day 35: Exodus 34–36; Matthew 23:1–22

Day 36: Exodus 37–38; Matthew 23:23–39

Day 37: Exodus 39–40; Matthew 24:1–22

Day 38: Leviticus 1–3; Matthew 24:23–51

Day 39: Leviticus 4–6; Matthew 25:1–30

Day 40: Leviticus 7–9; Matthew 25:31–46

Day 41: Leviticus 10–12; Matthew 26:1–19

Day 42: Leviticus 13; Matthew 26:20–54

Day 43: Leviticus 14; Matthew 26:55–75

Day 44: Leviticus 15–17; Matthew 27:1–31

Day 45: Leviticus 18–19; Matthew 27:32–66

Day 46: Leviticus 20–21; Matthew 28:1–20

Day 47: Leviticus 22–23; Mark 1:1–22

Day 48: Leviticus 24–25; Mark 1:23–45

Day 49: Leviticus 26–27; Mark 2

Day 50: Numbers 1–2; Mark 3:1–21

Day 51: Numbers 3–4; Mark 3:22–35

Day 52: Numbers 5–6; Mark 4:1–20

Day 53: Numbers 7; Mark 4:21–41

Day 54: Numbers 8–10; Mark 5:1–20

Day 55: Numbers 11–13; Mark 5:21–43

Day 56: Numbers 14–15; Mark 6:1–32

Day 57: Numbers 16–17; Mark 6:33–56

Day 58: Numbers 18–20; Mark 7:1–13

Day 59: Numbers 21–22; Mark 7:14–37

Day 60: Numbers 23–25; Mark 8:1–21

Day 61: Numbers 26–27; Mark 8:22–38

Day 62: Numbers 28–29; Mark 9:1–29

Day 63: Numbers 30–31; Mark 9:30–50

Day 64: Numbers 32–33; Mark 10:1–31

Day 65: Numbers 34–36; Mark 10:32–52

Day 66: Deuteronomy 1–2; Mark 11:1–19

Day 67: Deuteronomy 3–4; Mark 11:20–33

Day 68: Deuteronomy 5–7; Mark 12:1–27

Day 69: Deuteronomy 8–10; Mark 12:28–44

Day 70: Deuteronomy 11–13; Mark 13:1–13

Day 71: Deuteronomy 14–16; Mark 13:14–37

Day 72: Deuteronomy 17–19; Mark 14:1–25

Day 73: Deuteronomy 20–22; Mark 14:26–50

Day 74: Deuteronomy 23–25; Mark 14:51–72

Day 75: Deuteronomy 26–27; Mark 15:1–26

Day 76: Deuteronomy 28; Mark 15:27–47

Day 77: Deuteronomy 29–30; Mark 16

Day 78: Deuteronomy 31–32; Luke 1:1–23

Day 79: Deuteronomy 33–34; Luke 1:24–56

Day 80: Joshua 1–3; Luke 1:57–80

Day 81: Joshua 4–6; Luke 2:1–24

Day 82: Joshua 7–8; Luke 2:25–52

Day 83: Joshua 9–10; Luke 3

Day 84: Joshua 11–13; Luke 4:1–32

Day 85: Joshua 14–15; Luke 4:33–44

Day 86: Joshua 16–18; Luke 5:1–16

Day 87: Joshua 19–20; Luke 5:17–39

Day 88: Joshua 21–22; Luke 6:1–26

Day 89: Joshua 23–24; Luke 6:27–49

Day 90: Judges 1–2; Luke 7:1–30

Day 91: Judges 3–5; Luke 7:31–50

Day 92: Judges 6–7; Luke 8:1–21

Day 93: Judges 8–9; Luke 8:22–56

Day 94: Judges 10–11; Luke 9:1–36

Day 95: Judges 12–14; Luke 9:37–62

Day 96: Judges 15–17; Luke 10:1–24

Day 97: Judges 18–19; Luke 10:25–42

Day 98: Judges 20–21; Luke 11:1–28

Day 99: Ruth 1–4; Luke 11:29–54

Day 100: 1 Samuel 1–3; Luke 12:1–34

Day 101: 1 Samuel 4–6; Luke 12:35–59

Day 102: 1 Samuel 7–9; Luke 13:1–21

Day 103: 1 Samuel 10–12; Luke 13:22–35

Day 104: 1 Samuel 13–14; Luke 14:1–24

Day 105: 1 Samuel 15–16; Luke 14:25–35

Day 106: 1 Samuel 17–18; Luke 15:1–10

Day 107: 1 Samuel 19–21; Luke 15:11–32

Day 108: 1 Samuel 22–24; Luke 16:1–18

Day 109: 1 Samuel 25–26; Luke 16:19–31

Day 110: 1 Samuel 27–29; Luke 17:1–19

Day 111: 1 Samuel 30–31; Luke 17:20–37

Day 112: 2 Samuel 1–3; Luke 18:1–17

Day 113: 2 Samuel 4–6; Luke 18:18–43

Day 114: 2 Samuel 7–9; Luke 19:1–28

Day 115: 2 Samuel 10–12; Luke 19:29–48

Day 116: 2 Samuel 13–14; Luke 20:1–26

Day 117: 2 Samuel 15–16; Luke 20:27–47

Day 118: 2 Samuel 17–18; Luke 21:1–19

Day 119: 2 Samuel 19–20; Luke 21:20–38

Day 120: 2 Samuel 21–22; Luke 22:1–30

Day 121: 2 Samuel 23–24; Luke 22:31–53

Day 122: 1 Kings 1–2; Luke 22:54–71

Day 123: 1 Kings 3–5; Luke 23:1–26

Day 124: 1 Kings 6–7; Luke 23:27–38

Day 125: 1 Kings 8–9; Luke 23:39–56

Day 126: 1 Kings 10–11; Luke 24:1–35

Day 127: 1 Kings 12–13; Luke 24:36–53

Day 128: 1 Kings 14–15; John 1:1–28

Day 129: 1 Kings 16–18; John 1:29–51

Day 130: 1 Kings 19–20; John 2

Day 131: 1 Kings 21–22; John 3:1–21

Day 132: 2 Kings 1–3; John 3:22–36

Day 133: 2 Kings 4–5; John 4:1–30

Day 134: 2 Kings 6–8; John 4:31–54

Day 135: 2 Kings 9–11; John 5:1–24

Day 136: 2 Kings 12–14; John 5:25–47

Day 137: 2 Kings 15–17; John 6:1–21

Day 138: 2 Kings 18–19; John 6:22–44

Day 139: 2 Kings 20–22; John 6:45–71

Day 140: 2 Kings 23–25; John 7:1–31

Day 141: 1 Chronicles 1–2; John 7:32–53

Day 142: 1 Chronicles 3–5; John 8:1–20

Day 143: 1 Chronicles 6–7; John 8:21–36

Day 144: 1 Chronicles 8–10; John 8:37–59

Day 145: 1 Chronicles 11–13; John 9:1–23

Day 146: 1 Chronicles 14–16; John 9:24–41

Day 147: 1 Chronicles 17–19; John 10:1–21

Day 148: 1 Chronicles 20–22; John 10:22–42

Day 149: 1 Chronicles 23–25; John 11:1–17

Day 150: 1 Chronicles 26–27; John 11:18–46

Day 151: 1 Chronicles 28–29; John 11:47–57

Day 152: 2 Chronicles 1–3; John 12:1–19

Day 153: 2 Chronicles 4–6; John 12:20–50

Day 154: 2 Chronicles 7–9; John 13:1–17

Day 155: 2 Chronicles 10–12; John 13:18–38

Day 156: 2 Chronicles 13–16; John 14

Day 157: 2 Chronicles 17–19; John 15

Day 158: 2 Chronicles 20–22; John 16:1–15

Day 159: 2 Chronicles 23–25; John 16:16–33

Day 160: 2 Chronicles 26–28; John 17

Day 161: 2 Chronicles 29–31; John 18:1–23

Day 162: 2 Chronicles 32–33; John 18:24–40

Day 163: 2 Chronicles 34–36; John 19:1–22

Day 164: Ezra 1–2; John 19:23–42

Day 165: Ezra 3–5; John 20

Day 166: Ezra 6–8; John 21

Day 167: Ezra 9–10; Acts 1

Day 168: Nehemiah 1–2; Acts 2:1–13

Day 169: Nehemiah 4–6; Acts 2:14–47

Day 170: Nehemiah 7–8; Acts 3

Day 171: Nehemiah 9–11; Acts 4:1–22

Day 172: Nehemiah 12–13; Acts 4:23–37

Day 173: Esther 1–3; Acts 5:1–16

Day 174: Esther 4–6; Acts 5:17–42

Day 175: Esther 7–10; Acts 6

Day 176: Job 1–3; Acts 7:1–19

Day 177: Job 4–6; Acts 7:20–43

Day 178: Job 7–9; Acts 7:44–60

Day 179: Job 10–12; Acts 8:1–25

Day 180: Job 13–15; Acts 8:26–40

Day 181: Job 16–18; Acts 9:1–22

Day 182: Job 19–20; Acts 9:23–43

Day 183: Job 21–22; Acts 10:1–23

Day 184: Job 23–25; Acts 10:24–48

Day 185: Job 26–28; Acts 11

Day 186: Job 29–30; Acts 12

Day 187: Job 31–32; Acts 13:1–23

Day 188: Job 33–34; Acts 13:24–52

Day 189: Job 35–37; Acts 14

Day 190: Job 38–39; Acts 15:1–21

Day 191: Job 40–42; Acts 15:22–41

Day 192: Psalms 1–3; Acts 16:1–15

Day 193: Psalms 4–6; Acts 16:16–40

Day 194: Psalms 7–9; Acts 17:1–15

Day 195: Psalms 10–12; Acts 17:16–34

Day 196: Psalms 13–16; Acts 18

Day 197: Psalms 17–18; Acts 19:1–20

Day 198: Psalms 19–21; Acts 19:21–41

Day 199: Psalms 22–24; Acts 20:1–16

Day 200: Psalms 25–27; Acts 20:17–38

Day 201: Psalms 28–30; Acts 21:1–14

Day 202: Psalms 31–33; Acts 21:15–40

Day 203: Psalm 34–35; Acts 22

Day 204: Psalms 36–37; Acts 23:1–11

Day 205: Psalms 38–40; Acts 23:12–35

Day 206: Psalms 41–43; Acts 24

Day 207: Psalms 44–46; Acts 25

Day 208: Psalms 47–49; Acts 26

Day 209: Psalms 50–52; Acts 27:1–25

Day 210: Psalms 53–55; Acts 27:26–44

Day 211: Psalms 56–58; Acts 28:1–15

Day 212: Psalms 59–61; Acts 28:16–31

Day 213: Psalms 62–64; Romans 1

Day 214: Psalms 65–67; Romans 2

Day 215: Psalms 68–69; Romans 3

Day 216: Psalms 70–72; Romans 4

Day 217: Psalms 73–74; Romans 5

Day 218: Psalms 75–77; Romans 6

Day 219: Psalm 78; Romans 7

Day 220: Psalms 79–81; Romans 8:1–18

Day 221: Psalms 82–84; Romans 8:19–39

Day 222: Psalms 85–87; Romans 9

Day 223: Psalms 88–89; Romans 10

Day 224: Psalms 90–92; Romans 11:1–21

Day 225: Psalms 93–95; Romans 11:22–36

Day 226: Psalms 96–98; Romans 12

Day 227: Psalms 99–102; Romans 13

Day 228: Psalms 103–104; Romans 14

Day 229: Psalms 105–106; Romans 15:1–20

Day 230: Psalms 107–108; Romans 15:21–33

Day 231: Psalms 109–111; Romans 16

Day 232: Psalms 112–115; 1 Corinthians 1

Day 233: Psalms 116–118; 1 Corinthians 2

Day 234: Psalms 119:1–48; 1 Corinthians 3

Day 235: Psalms 119:49–104; 1 Corinthians 4

Day 236: Psalms 119:105–176; 1 Corinthians 5

Day 237: Psalms 120–123; 1 Corinthians 6

Day 238: Psalms 124–127; 1 Corinthians 7:1–24

Day 239: Psalms 128–131; 1 Corinthians 7:25–40

Day 240: Psalms 132–135; 1 Corinthians 8

Day 241: Psalms 136–138; 1 Corinthians 9

Day 242: Psalms 139–141; 1 Corinthians 10:1–13

Day 243: Psalms 142–144; 1 Corinthians 10:14–33

Day 244: Psalms 145–147; 1 Corinthians 11:1–15

Day 245: Psalms 148–150; 1 Corinthians 11:16–34

Day 246: Proverbs 1–2; 1 Corinthians 12

Day 247: Proverbs 3–4; 1 Corinthians 13

Day 248: Proverbs 5–6; 1 Corinthians 14:1–20

Day 249: Proverbs 7–8; 1 Corinthians 14:21–40

Day 250: Proverbs 9–10; 1 Corinthians 15:1–32

Day 251: Proverbs 11–12; 1 Corinthians 15:33–58

Day 252: Proverbs 13–14; 1 Corinthians 16

Day 253: Proverbs 15–16; 2 Corinthians 1

Day 254: Proverbs 17–18; 2 Corinthians 2

Day 255: Proverbs 19–20; 2 Corinthians 3

Day 256: Proverbs 21–22; 2 Corinthians 4

Day 257: Proverbs 23–24; 2 Corinthians 5

Day 258: Proverbs 25–27; 2 Corinthians 6

Day 259: Proverbs 28–29; 2 Corinthians 7

Day 260: Proverbs 30–31; 2 Corinthians 8

Day 261: Ecclesiastes 1–3; 2 Corinthians 9

Day 262: Ecclesiastes 4–6; 2 Corinthians 10

Day 263: Ecclesiastes 7–9; 2 Corinthians 11:1–15

Day 264: Ecclesiastes 10–12; 2 Corinthians 11:16–33

Day 265: Song of Solomon 1–3; 2 Corinthians 12

Day 266: Song of Solomon 4–5; 2 Corinthians 13

Day 267: Song of Solomon 6–8; Galatians 1

Day 268: Isaiah 1–3; Galatians 2

Day 269: Isaiah 4–6; Galatians 3

Day 270: Isaiah 7–9; Galatians 4

Day 271: Isaiah 10–12; Galatians 5

Day 272: Isaiah 13–15; Galatians 6

Day 273: Isaiah 16–18; Ephesians 1

Day 274: Isaiah 19–21; Ephesians 2

Day 275: Isaiah 22–23; Ephesians 3

Day 276: Isaiah 24–26; Ephesians 4

Day 277: Isaiah 27–28; Ephesians 5

Day 278: Isaiah 29–30; Ephesians 6

Day 279: Isaiah 31–33; Philippians 1

Day 280: Isaiah 34–36; Philippians 2

Day 281: Isaiah 37–38; Philippians 3

Day 282: Isaiah 39–40; Philippians 4

Day 283: Isaiah 41–42; Colossians 1

Day 284: Isaiah 43–44; Colossians 2

Day 285: Isaiah 45–47; Colossians 3

Day 286: Isaiah 48–49; Colossians 4

Day 287: Isaiah 50–52; 1 Thessalonians 1

Day 288: Isaiah 53–55; 1 Thessalonians 2

Day 289: Isaiah 56–58; 1 Thessalonians 3

Day 290: Isaiah 59–61; 1 Thessalonians 4

Day 291: Isaiah 62–64; 1 Thessalonians 5

Day 292: Isaiah 65–66; 2 Thessalonians 1

Day 293: Jeremiah 1–2; 2 Thessalonians 2

Day 294: Jeremiah 3–4; 2 Thessalonians 3

Day 295: Jeremiah 5–6; 1 Timothy 1

Day 296: Jeremiah 7–8; 1 Timothy 2

Day 297: Jeremiah 9–10; 1 Timothy 3

Day 298: Jeremiah 11–13; 1 Timothy 4

Day 299: Jeremiah 14–16; 1 Timothy 5

Day 300: Jeremiah 17–19; 1 Timothy 6

Day 301: Jeremiah 20–22; 2 Timothy 1

Day 302: Jeremiah 23–24; 2 Timothy 2

Day 303: Jeremiah 25–26; 2 Timothy 3

Day 304: Jeremiah 27–28; 2 Timothy 4

Day 305: Jeremiah 29–30; Titus 1

Day 306: Jeremiah 31–32; Titus 2

Day 307: Jeremiah 33–35; Titus 3

Day 308: Jeremiah 36–37; Philemon 1

Day 309: Jeremiah 38–39; Hebrews 1

Day 310: Jeremiah 40–42; Hebrews 2

Day 311: Jeremiah 43–45; Hebrews 3

Day 312: Jeremiah 46–48; Hebrews 4

Day 313: Jeremiah 49–50; Hebrews 5

Day 314: Jeremiah 51–52; Hebrews 6

Day 315: Lamentations 1–2; Hebrews 7

Day 316: Lamentations 3–5; Hebrews 8

Day 317: Ezekiel 1–3; Hebrews 9

Day 318: Ezekiel 4–6; Hebrews 10:1–23

Day 319: Ezekiel 7–9; Hebrews 10:24–39

Day 320: Ezekiel 10–12; Hebrews 11:1–19

Day 321: Ezekiel 13–15; Hebrews 11:20–40

Day 322: Ezekiel 16; Hebrews 12

Day 323: Ezekiel 17–19; Hebrews 13

Day 324: Ezekiel 20–21; James 1

Day 325: Ezekiel 22–23; James 2

Day 326: Ezekiel 24–26; James 3

Day 327: Ezekiel 27–28; James 4

Day 328: Ezekiel 29–31; James 5

Day 329: Ezekiel 32–33; 1 Peter 1

Day 330: Ezekiel 34–35; 1 Peter 2

Day 331: Ezekiel 36–37; 1 Peter 3

Day 332: Ezekiel 38–39; 1 Peter 4

Day 333: Ezekiel 40; 1 Peter 5

Day 334: Ezekiel 41–42; 2 Peter 1

Day 335: Ezekiel 43–44; 2 Peter 2

Day 336: Ezekiel 45–46; 2 Peter 3

Day 337: Ezekiel 47–48; 1 John 1

Day 338: Daniel 1–2; 1 John 2

Day 339: Daniel 3–4; 1 John 3

Day 340: Daniel 5–6; 1 John 4

Day 341: Daniel 7–8; 1 John 5

Day 342: Daniel 9–10; 2 John 1

Day 343: Daniel 11–12; 3 John 1

Day 344: Hosea 1–4; Jude 1

Day 345: Hosea 5–8; Revelation 1

Day 346: Hosea 9–11; Revelation 2

Day 347: Hosea 12–14; Revelation 3

Day 348: Joel 1–3; Revelation 4

Day 349: Amos 1–3; Revelation 5

Day 350: Amos 4–6; Revelation 6

Day 351: Amos 7–9; Revelation 7

Day 352: Obadiah 1; Revelation 8

Day 353: Jonah 1–4; Revelation 9

Day 354: Micah 1–3; Revelation 10

Day 355: Micah 4–5; Revelation 11

Day 356: Micah 6–7; Revelation 12

Day 357: Nahum 1–3; Revelation 13

Day 358: Habakkuk 1–3; Revelation 14

Day 359: Zephaniah; Revelation 15

Day 360: Haggai 1–2; Revelation 16

Day 361: Zechariah 1–3; Revelation 17

Day 362: Zechariah 4–6; Revelation 18

Day 363: Zechariah 7–9; Revelation 19

Day 364: Zechariah 10–12; Revelation 20

Day 365: Zechariah 13–14; Revelation 21

Day 366: Malachi 1–4; Revelation 22

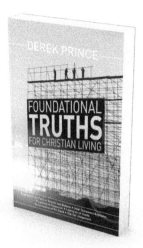

FOUNDATIONAL TRUTHS FOR CHRISTIAN LIVING

Develop a strong, balanced, Spirit-filled life, by discovering the foundations of faith: salvation; baptism, the Holy Spirit, laying on hands, the believers' resurrection and eternal judgment.

Its reader-friendly format includes a comprehensive index of topics and a complete index of Scripture verses used in the book.

£13.99
ISBN 978-1-908594-82-2

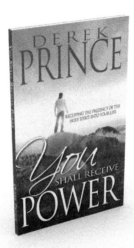

YOU SHALL RECEIVE POWER

- Discover the Holy Spirit's role as a Guide and learn how to be led by the Spirit, how to hear God's voice and how to cooperate with the Holy Spirit's working in our life.
- Derek Prince thoroughly examines what the Word of God teaches on the the baptism in the Holy Spirit and helps you learn how to be led by the Spirit, how to live in God's grace and how to hear God's voice.

£6.99
ISBN 978-1-78263-442-3

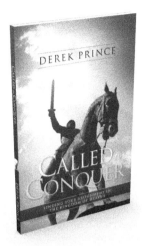

CALLED TO CONQUER

- Do you want to know the job, the place, the relationships and the ministry God has ordained for you?
- Do you want to enter that special place of provision, responsibility and privilege designed just for you – in this life and into eternity?
- Are you willing to answer God's call?

Then you are ready to discover God's calling for your life. It is not complicated and it is intensely practical. With a thorough examination of Old and New Testament passages, Derek shows you what a calling is, the specific gifts God gives, steps to finding your place in God's service and much more.

£7.99
ISBN 978-1-901144-57-4

www.dpmuk.org/shop

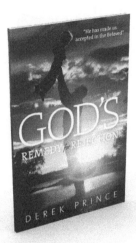

GOD'S REMEDY FOR REJECTION

Rejection is an all too common experience, but it can cause permanent spiritual wounds.

In our society, millions of people have experienced rejection as a result of divorce, child abuse, parental neglect, poverty, public humiliation, failure at school or work, and more.

Discover how to apply God's remedy for rejection to your heart and leave the effect of rejection behind permanently!

£2.99
ISBN 978-1-908594-63-1

CORRESPONDENCE COURSE

If you have enjoyed this study and would like to deepen your knowledge of God's Word and apply the teaching – why not enrol on Derek Prince's Christian Foundations Bible Course?

Building on the Foundations of God's Word

A detailed study of the six essential doctrines of Christianity found in Hebrews 6:1–2.

- Scripture-based curriculum
- Practical, personal application
- Systematic Scripture memorisation
- Opportunity for questions and personal feedback from course tutor
- Certificate upon completion
- Modular based syllabus
- Set your own pace
- Affordable

Based on Foundation Truths for Christian Living

For a prospectus, application form and pricing information, please visit www.dpmuk.org, call 01462 492100 or send an e-mail to enquiries@dpmuk.org

MORE BEST-SELLERS
BY DEREK PRINCE

www.dpmuk.org/shop

DPM OFFICES WORLDWIDE

DPM – Asia/Pacific
38 Hawdon Street
Sydenham
Christchurch 8023
New Zealand
T: + 64 3 366 4443
E: admin@dpm.co.nz
W: www.dpm.co.nz and www.derekprince.in

DPM – Australia
15 Park Road
Seven Hills
New South Wales 2147
Australia
T: +61 2 9838 7778
E: enquiries@au.derekprince.com
W: www.derekprince.com.au

DPM – Canada
P.O. Box 8354 Halifax
Nova Scotia B3K 5M1
Canada
T: + 1 902 443 9577
E: enquiries.dpm@eastlink.ca
W: www.derekprince.org

DPM – France
B.P. 31, Route d'Oupia
34210 Olonzac
France
T: + 33 468 913872
E: info@derekprince.fr
W: www.derekprince.fr

DPM – Germany
Söldenhofstr. 10
83308 Trostberg
Germany
T: + 49 8621 64146
E: ibl@ibl-dpm.net
W: www.ibl-dpm.net

DPM – Netherlands
Nijverheidsweg 12
7005 BJ Doetinchem
Netherlands
T: +31 251–255044
E: info@derekprince.nl
W: www.derekprince.nl

DPM – Norway
P.O. Box 129
Lodderfjord
N-5881 Bergen
Norway
T: +47 928 39855
E: sverre@derekprince.no
W: www.derekprince.no

Derek Prince Publications Pte. Ltd.
P.O. Box 2046
Robinson Road Post Office
Singapore 904046
T: + 65 6392 1812
E: dpmchina@singnet.com.sg
W: www.dpmchina.org (English)
www.ygmweb.org (Chinese)

DPM – South Africa
P.O. Box 33367
Glenstantia
0010 Pretoria
South Africa
T: +27 12 348 9537
E: enquiries@derekprince.co.za
W: www.derekprince.co.za

DPM – Switzerland
Alpenblick 8
CH-8934 Knonau
Switzerland
T: + 41 44 768 25 06
E: dpm-ch@ibl-dpm.net
W: www.ibl-dpm.net

DPM – UK
PO Box 393
Hitchin SG5 9EU
United Kingdom
T: + 44 1462 492100
E: enquiries@dpmuk.org
W: www.dpmuk.org

DPM – USA
P.O. Box 19501
Charlotte NC 28219
USA
T: + 1 704 357 3556
E: ContactUs@derekprince.org
W: www.derekprince.org